Towns and Villages
OF ENGLAND

LYME REGIS

To Abe and Marion

a memento of their visit
here

It was great to help
you for this part of your
trip

Love   Audrey & Pat

April 1996

Towns and Villages
OF ENGLAND

LYME REGIS

TED GOSLING AND
LYN MARSHALL

ALAN SUTTON

First published in the United Kingdom in 1993 by
Alan Sutton Publishing Limited
Phoenix Mill · Far Thrupp · Stroud · Gloucestershire

First published in the United States of America in 1993 by
Alan Sutton Publishing Inc
83 Washington Street · Dover · NH 03820

British Library Cataloguing in Publication Data

A catalogue record for this book is available from the British Library

ISBN 0-7509-0570–0

Typeset in 11/13 Bembo.
Typesetting and origination by
Alan Sutton Publishing Limited.
Printed and bound in Great Britain by
Hartnolls Ltd, Bodmin, Cornwall.

Contents

Introduction

As Town Crier and the conductor of the historical tours of Lyme Regis, I have had to study in detail the history of this ancient seaport. I therefore deem it a great honour to be asked by fellow historians Ted Gosling and Lyn Marshall to write the introduction to what is a definitive and concise history of Lyme Regis. With this photographic record they have preserved many memories of the town affectionately known as 'The Pearl of Dorset'.

Embarking on the monumental task of recording in one volume the momentous events, colourful characters, disasters and triumphs that have helped to establish the charm of Lyme Regis must have been a daunting prospect. However, between them Ted Gosling and Lyn Marshall have skilfully collated a very illuminating book, spanning over a thousand years.

Lyn Marshall has a keen interest in the history of the area, and Ted Gosling's period as curator of the Philpot Museum gave him a unique opportunity to study the character of a town with a fierce civic pride. This is still evident today in an indigenous population steeped in the tradition of a rebellious and dissenting spirit.

Mr Gosling and Mrs Marshall's book will be a welcome addition to the works of other historians of Lyme Regis, including Roberts, Wanklyn and Fowles.

Congratulations on a job well done.

Richard Fox
Lyme Regis Town Crier 1977–93
(Three times World Champion and four times Best-dressed Crier)

CHAPTER ONE

The Early Days

It is almost certain from Domesday Book records (1086) that there was a small but thriving settlement at Lyme Regis by the end of the eleventh century and that at its centre was a small community of monks at Lyme Abbas. The local inhabitants found enough work to make a living. Farming was, of course, important, and, with the sea on the doorstep, fishing and salt manufacture provided employment.

There was at least one mill, 'on Belet's land', but it is safe to assume that the swift-flowing Lym offered its waters to more than one mill between Uplyme and its outlet into the English Channel. The existence of salt-works meant that there was commercial exchange with other communities, contact with whom would have been along such roads that existed out of the town. Today's modern road through Charmouth was once part of the Roman Icknield Way, skirting modern Lyme Regis before going up Clappentail, off to Seaton, arguably Roman Moridunum, on to Beer, where stone was quarried, and then to Isca (Exeter). For much of the way it is now followed by the modern road through Rousdon, Colyford and Sidford. Northwards, to Axminster and Crewkerne, Lyme's merchants had to take the road that followed the tiny Lym up towards Hunters' Lodge, much as it does today. Little is known of early life in Lyme Regis but, from an entry in the Patent Rolls of 1254, in which Henry III commanded the bailiffs at Lyme to impress ships to carry his queen and son (later Edward I) to Gascony, it seems highly probable that The Cobb was already in existence. Without it there would have been no shelter on Lyme's largely inhospitable coast for ships of a sufficient size to carry the royal party.

The Cobb was a great boon to local fishermen and probably owes its existence to their needs. That the fishermen went far afield is suggested by a running feud that sprang up between them and the fishermen of Dartmouth. This difference of opinion became so out of hand that Henry III sent a writ to the bailiffs demanding that they should seek evidence to 'identify the perpetrators of many enormous transgressions upon the seas' between them. Sadly, nothing is known of the outcome. Although the granting of a fair and market by Henry III in 1271 need not necessarily imply that there was considerable trade in the town, it does suggest the growing importance of the

1

Sherborne Lane, *c.* 1908. This lane is so named because of the association of Lyme with the monks of Sherborne Abbey. Lyme Abbas was sited here, and it was in this area that the monks boiled the sea water for salt

place. Then, as now, however, there were always people who would try to take advantage of the system. For example, Elias de Rabayne tried holding a market on every day of the week rather than just Mondays as granted in the charter. When he was taken to court it was found that he never had the authority for a market in the first place.

Elias had come into possession of estates including Lyme Regis, and others in Norfolk and Lincolnshire, rather in the manner in which he tried to 'establish' his own market in the town. During the reign of Henry III the estates had belonged to Stephen de Bayeux. When Stephen died they passed into the custody of the king. There were two heiresses, the daughters Matilda and Joan. The king, who seemed no judge of character in this case, granted the wardship to Elias, with, of course, the right to say whom the girls could marry. He quickly made sure of half of the inheritance for himself by marrying the elder daughter, Matilda, and went on to appropriate the other half after marrying off Joan to a Picardian by the name of Baudrat. Henry was not amused and seized the estates, taking Elias's own estates as well for good measure. Thus half of Lyme came into the king's hands. Edward I later acquired the Lyme lands of Glastonbury Abbey. As a result it became a royal manor and was named Lyme Regis.

In a letter from Edward I to the Count and Countess of Flanders in May 1297 he says that he was staying in Lyme, and in good health. Edward granted Lyme its first charter in 1284 and a second followed a year later. This marked an important step in the town's development – the grant of borough status, bringing with it a voice in Parliament by two burgesses who, when they attended, would have their expenses paid by the town. Direct representation in Parliament, which began with William Tuluse and Geofrey le Qeu, did not end until 1832. On their return from London the MPs handed in a 'writ de expensis' to the mayor and bailiffs, each getting 2s. per day, but being left in little doubt that the less time they spent in Parliament, the happier Lyme would be. A merchant guild was also granted, an institution that would govern all of the town's commercial activities, including the market.

Medieval boroughs such as Lyme prized and jealously guarded their liberties and free customs, especially the right to hold their own local courts instead of the inconvenience of having to attend the shire courts, and a hustings was held at Lyme once a week. There was also more freedom in the management of their local affairs, direct access to the Crown and, perhaps most important of all, exemption from tolls and lastage (a fee payable by traders attending fairs and markets) when carrying their merchandise for trade, both at home and abroad. Not all boroughs enjoyed all of these privileges and, unusual for such a small town, Lyme was granted much the same liberties as the City of London. Lyme had a common seal for the business of the town, which depicts a ship at sea with a three-tailed pennon displaying the cross of St George on each tail. On one side of the mast can be seen the 'three lions passant gardant' of England; on the other are the arms of Edward I and Queen Eleanor. These details date the seal to between 1272 and 1290.

Edward II addressed a writ to the mayor and bailiffs of Lyme, ordering them to 'make a diligent search' for letters conveyed through Lyme, either going to or coming from abroad. He knew of the treason being hatched by his wife, Queen Isabella, and her lover, Roger de Mortimer, and was searching for proof. By then (1327), however, it was already too late: Edward was deposed later that year and then murdered. The first historical reference to The Cobb is in a document of 1328, in a petition to King Edward III from the burgesses of Lyme. It says that the town was 'situated on the sea where no harbour or place to secure ships existed, except a certain work called "Le Cobbe", built of timber and rocks, which was beat down and quite destroyed by the violence of the seas'. They went on to point out that they had no means of their own to rebuild the structure, and asked the king to give money towards the work. Eventually, in 1336, Edward III granted them the right to collect a penny from every pound on salt or any other goods leaving or entering Lyme. The 'tax' was to be collected for five years, and this was later extended by a further three years. It seems obvious that Lyme was already a port of some standing, a fact that was underlined in 1342 when the king ordered that two of the better and more discreet mariners of Lyme should attend Parliament to consult on the safety of the coast and its protection in case of invasion. By then, of course, England was well into the Hundred Years War.

It was in Edward III's reign that the burgesses of Lyme were granted, at fee-farm (an estate in land held on condition of homage and service to a superior lord) for an annual rent of thirty-two marks, certain rights, which included the rents of stalls and houses in the market, and toll of all items brought into the town for sale.

The fourteenth century was an uncertain time. Lyme, in particular, suffered first from the plague and then from the forces of nature. The Black Death reached England via the Dorset coast, and Lyme was among the early sufferers. The consequent decimation of the population of the country led to the king addressing an order to all seaports, including Lyme, that said:

> A considerable part of the population has died of the present pestilence and the exchequer is exhausted. Understanding that very many daily go abroad with all the money they can collect; and that if such departure be tolerated the kingdom will soon be destitute of men as well as money.

Edward therefore ordered bailiffs at the ports to stop anyone leaving unless he was a merchant or a messenger. Late in the reign of Edward III Lyme was devastated by a violent storm, which led to the townspeople petitioning the king for help. Lyme, they said, had been competently built when the burgesses had enjoyed their rights in fee-farm for ever for a thirty-two mark annual rent. Then it had been rich and prosperous, with many wealthy inhabitants, all contributing to the town's welfare and prosperity. A sudden storm at Martinmas had, however, left the town:

> in such a state that the greater part is carried away and laid waste by the fury and violence of the seas. The aforesaid rich merchants who bore the burden of the town are now dead. Almost all the survivors, with the exception of six or eight, have left the town for the above reason.

The Cobb had been totally ruined, leaving Lyme without contact by sea. This meant that, without the passage of goods, the townspeople were deprived of the means of paying the fee-farm to the king and they asked him to take Lyme into his own charge and waive any fee-farm arrears.

Richard II came to the throne and on 13 February 1377 issued a writ, ordering six men to investigate the damage and distress in the town. The ensuing report painted a harsh picture. Seventy-seven tenements in the town had been wasted and washed away; seventy-one more were empty either

The Medieval Lepers' Well by The Lynch

The Lepers' Well

because of the death of the merchants or owing to the survivors being forced to leave the town; fifteen large ships and as many as forty smaller vessels (half of them fishing boats) had been destroyed; and there would be a bill of £300 if The Cobb was to be repaired. The report went on to state that now only eight burgesses (all named) and twenty-one poor people were still living in the town, whose only income was from the market tolls, thus making the rebuilding of The Cobb a priority. Procrastination is not an invention of modern authority: it took Richard twelve years to make any answer to the report, and then all he did was to grant Lyme to William Merton, a local man, in fee-farm for ten years. A commission of enquiry found Lyme still in a desolate state as many as ten years later, and the fee-farm was reduced, but only for a few years.

Further petitions were made to King Henry IV, the first in 1403 when the burgesses complained not only about the state of the town, but also of the danger of invasion by the French. Lyme, along with other towns on the Devon and Dorset Channel coasts, had been burned by the French during the previous reign, and the king was reminded that it was essential to have the town fully inhabited again to 'resist the malice of the enemies'. They prayed for release from the fee-farm arrears, and to pay such a rent as they could fairly pay 'as a deed of charity . . . as a relief to the poor burgesses . . . and to cause the town to be more thickly inhabited'.

Lyme recovered, with or without the king's help, and it appeared to be a prosperous little place again by 1553, at the start of Mary I's reign, when the new queen granted a weekly market on Fridays, as well as two fairs – one in February and the other in October. She also granted all the tolls and customs of the fairs and markets, but Lyme lost a grant of £20 per annum made in the reign of Henry VIII towards the upkeep of The Cobb.

This prosperity continued in Elizabeth I's reign, when probably the best-known of Lyme's MPs, Sir Francis Walsingham, the queen's foreign secretary, represented the town from 1563 to 1567. Walsingham employed a local man, Arthur Gregory, as one of his better agents, who, it was said, 'had the admirable talent of forcing the Seal of a letter, yet so invisibly that it still appeared a virgin to the exactest beholder. Secretary Walsingham made great use of him.' That use included being placed near Mary Queen of Scots and helping to unravel the Babington Conspiracy, which hastened Mary's execution. Gregory also worked for Robert Cecil, Walsingham's successor, and had a hand in deciphering a letter connected with the Gunpowder Plot. He retired in around 1608, coming back to live in his native Lyme where he found temporary, and perhaps obvious, employment as a 'searcher of customs'. He went on to become mayor, and it was during his time in office that the use of Portland stone in work on The Cobb is first mentioned. Gregory's last mark on the history of his home town was in August 1622, when he was fined 6s. 8d. for making a disrespectful (and, sadly, unknown) remark about his successor as mayor.

Differences of opinion between those in authority in the town were not uncommon, as is true today. Queen Elizabeth I had been asked by the townspeople to end the dissension and, with that aim in mind, had granted a charter in 1591, which laid down that there should be 'a common council consisting of the mayor and six of the most honest and discreet burgesses'. The mayor was chosen by the 'Capital Burgesses' (the most important freeholders in the town) and the Common Council, and the honest six by an unspecified procedure. Another document, dated 1583, explained how the freemen and free burgesses acquired the freedom of the borough. The document was described as 'A Table conteyning as well the Rates of the accustomed Duties payable to the Use and Mayntenance of the Towne and Cob of Lyme Regis as also divers other things concerning the ffraunchises and Liberties of the same Towne '. It stated that all those who had freehold in the 'Burrough' would have the freedom of the town and were made free by a fine and then an oath, thus becoming 'ffree Burgesses'. Those who paid the fine and took the oath but did not have a freehold in the town were simply 'ffreemen'.

Cobb duties were considerable and were specified in the document as follows:

Sweet Wynes, Oyles & Sack per Tonne .... 8d.
Gascoigine Wines per Tonne .... 6d.

Lynin Cloth per ffardell .... 3d.
Woollen Cloth per pack .... 3d.
All other gross wares per tonne .... 6d.
Killage of ev'ry Ship, Barque or Vessell .... 6d.
The same Ship, Barque or Vessell having a Boate .... 1s. 0d.
Itm. this p'ved in the said Inquision that in
Anno 1553 was rec'd for Ballast...1s. 0d.

   The mayoral accounts for Lyme Regis in the years around 1650 mention
payments of 12s. to 14s. a year to an official with the title of 'dog whipper'.
During this period almost every countryman possessed a dog, and it was a
common thing for worshippers to take their dogs to church with them. In
rural districts, where the parish was extensive and some of the worshippers
lived in farms some distance away from church, the farmer would take his
sheepdog with him and look after his flocks by the way. Naturally it
happened that now and again unseemly scenes occurred, and then the dog
whipper, armed with long wooden tongs and a whip, would intervene and
the disturber of the peace would be ejected as quietly as possible.
   Having survived the ups and downs of its fortunes, by the end of the
seventeenth century Lyme had developed into a stable and successful town
with a properly constituted council. The town's main income came through
The Cobb, and goods that passed through the port during the reign of Henry
VIII included wood, alum, honey, raisins, madder, wax, saffron, oil, tallow,
wine, canvas, iron and bow-staves. Trade was both local and cross-Channel
and there is evidence of regular trade with Morlaix in Brittany, as well as
more exotic goods being imported from the West Indies.

CHAPTER TWO

The Fane Influence, 1735–1835

The economic life and prosperity of Lyme Regis had always been dependent on trade, by land and sea, and on local industries. Both of these activities were steadily expanding, until there was a period of depression from 1730 to 1780.

Documentary evidence makes it clear that the kings and queens of England were aware of the existence of the Port of Lyme as early as the reign of Henry III, and that it was important enough in those days for them repeatedly to spend money on its maintenance. Even as late as 1824 the government spent thousands of pounds on the rebuilding of The Cobb. Figures indicating the volume of shipping using The Cobb harbour during the seventeenth century take the form of the value of the import duties paid at Lyme. During the reign of James I customs amounting to £5,000 per annum are recorded in the old Customs House papers, and a figure of £16,000 per annum was usual during the reign of Charles II. During the reign of James I, cargoes from Guinea, 'the Straits', the West Indies, Spain and Portugal were landed at Lyme. These imports included gold, ivory and, probably, sugar and tobacco. Towards the end of the seventeenth century Lyme traded with Newfoundland, Maryland, Virginia, Barbados, Malaga, Tangier, St Malo and Morlaix. Exports included woollens and linens made in Lyme. Cargoes for Bristol were often unloaded at The Cobb and transported further by land to avoid the dangers of the sea passage round Land's End.

The beginning of the war with France during the reign of William III coincided with the onset of a decline in the maritime trade of Lyme Regis. One reason for the latter was, indeed, the war, which seriously curtailed cross-Channel traffic. Another was the increase in the size of ships, as The Cobb harbour could not be used by ships of more than 150 tons, a size that had already been exceeded. A third was the end of the woollen and linen industries of Lyme, brought about by the Industrial Revolution and the northward drift of industry. This happened after about 1750 at the time Lyme was passing through its worst period of depression, when most of the people of Lyme were still employed in the woollen industry.

Although the decline in seaborne trade had been very serious, The Cobb harbour was still quite a busy place during the early nineteenth century.

Gun Cliff, 1832

Between 1800 and 1825 six hundred vessels a year berthed in The Cobb harbour, and in 1829 thirty-nine ships were owned at Lyme. Vessels of 80 tons maintained a regular fortnightly service between Lyme and the Port of London. A similar service between Lyme and the Channel Islands was maintained as late as 1851. This was a relic of the service that had supplied the garrisons of the Channel Islands during the Napoleonic Wars. In addition there was coastal traffic in coal and blue lias for the cement works near the harbour. Coal came to Lyme by sea until the arrival of the railway in 1903. The harbour was thus often quite crowded with such vessels. There was a shipbuilding yard close to the harbour, where a frigate had been built in 1654. One of the last ships built at Lyme was the 250 ton *Lyme Regis*, which was launched in 1849 by Lady Bayly.

The economic position of Lyme Regis was at its worst in around 1750, the population having decreased to less than a thousand. Land tax was badly in arrears. A petition to Parliament in 1772 asked for relief, stating that during the previous eighty years 117 houses had fallen into ruin. Many others had been burned down or washed away by the sea. Few of the larger houses had survived and no one would buy those that remained. Until 1758, when the turnpike was built, no road from Exeter to Charmouth and beyond passed through the town. The roads out from the town were mere lanes and were deeply rutted. Tradesmen travelling to London went in parties, on foot, having first made their wills! There were no houses close to The Cobb and only a few cottages to the west of Broad Street. The best of the remaining houses were the Great House in Broad Street, visited from time to time by the Earl of Chatham and his son William Pitt, and the house of Burridge, a merchant of the town, in the butter market.

Broad Street was chiefly inhabited by lacemakers, women who worked in the shade of their porches in summer weather, gossiping about the past glories of Lyme. Their lace was very fine, and they made a lace court dress here for Queen Charlotte. The best lace was sold for as much as five guineas a yard, at a time when the wages of labourers were only 4d. a day.

Little attention was paid to social distinctions, at least by those whose home was in Lyme. Children of rich and poor alike went to the same day-school. Everybody 'knew' everybody else, whatever his station in life. If a native of Lyme met another in difficulty in a 'foreign' town, he would help him out. This spirit was weakened when 'foreigners' who had no real interest in Lyme came to live in the town, making their living elsewhere and contributing nothing to local affairs.

Smuggling was common among all classes as the law was very lax. Smuggled liquor could not be seized once it had been taken above the high-water mark, so smugglers could leave pipes of wine on the beach, in full sight of The Customs House across the road from Cobb Gate. In about 1775 the town took on a new lease of life to become a fashionable watering-place, and a holiday resort it has continued to be ever since.

Early in the eighteenth century local government at Lyme Regis was blighted by the arrival of members of the Fane family, merchants of Bristol, under whose influence the town degenerated into a rotten, or pocket, borough.

From 1284, when Lyme Regis became a free borough, the town was represented in Parliament by two burgesses. The first member of the Fane family to become involved in Lyme Regis was Francis. His uncle, John Scrope of Bristol, was MP for Lyme from 1734, together with Henry Holt Henley, the lord of the manor. In 1754 Scrope died, Henley retired, and Francis Fane and his brother Thomas became members for Lyme.

The town's MPs were elected by the town council and freemen of Lyme, who were appointed by the council. To secure the nomination as the towns MPs, therefore, the Fanes first had to gain control of the town council. The freemen were the key. When Scrope first came to Lyme Regis there were 120 freemen, but later the Fanes saw to it that the number was limited to thirty or forty so that they could arrange to have a majority of freemen who favoured them, and could thereby manipulate the elections.

During the seventeenth century the rule had been that men who did not

A guest-house in Hill Road. It is here that the Earl of Westmorland stayed on his visits to the town

live in Lyme Regis could not become freemen, and the freedom they gained involved certain privileges. All of this was changed in 1703 when it became possible for non-residents to become freemen on payment of a small fee. This made it possible for the Fanes to become freemen and so 'pocket' the borough, as they only appeared in Lyme for election purposes.

By 1733 Francis Fane was on the town council, followed shortly by Thomas and Henry. By 1766 the Fanes were in so strong a position at Lyme that they could treat the townspeople with open contempt, as the following incident shows.

John Cartwright was an eminent supporter of the Parliamentary Reform movement. John was a naval officer commanding the revenue cutter *Sherborne* (involved in preventing smuggling), off the Portland station, when in 1766 he received and accepted an invitation to dine with the mayor and corporation of Lyme Regis at The Three Cups Hotel. After the wine had circulated with customary frequency Thomas Fane, the Earl of Westmorland and 'patron' of the town, was heard to say to importunate place-seekers, 'I have bought you all and by God I'll sell you all.' John's enthusiasm for Parliamentary Reform would not have been any the less for this experience.

During the period of Fane control the town suffered a great deal of neglect, and in 1778 some of the townsmen decided to try to rid themselves of their oppressors. The leaders of the revolt were Benjamin Follett, who was town clerk of Lyme Regis from 1735 until his death in 1792, and his sons, Thomas and John. They also had the support of three mayors of Lyme Regis.

Any three members of the town council were empowered to conduct routine business, but a 'corporate act' or important business required the presence of nine members. Giles Davie, an opponent of the Fanes, was allowed to become mayor for 1777/8, but as the Fane party were in the majority on the council they were able to confine Davie and his party to routine business merely by staying away from council meetings. Matters came to a head when they continually ignored summonses to attend to important business and 'Articles of Complaint' were exhibited against six members of the Fane party. The main complaints were that they 'wilfully absented' themselves from Lyme Regis and 'wilfully omitted and neglected the duty and execution of office', which caused 'great hindrance and delay' to the business of the mayor and government of the town. They were ousted from the council, followed by two more members a month later. These were not valid actions, as illegal freemen were allowed to vote. The Fanes appealed to the High Court against the decision and won their case. Further 'Articles of Complaint' were exhibited, but the Fanes invariably won on appeal.

The Assembly Rooms and Bell Cliff, 1814

In spite of the strenuous efforts of the Folletts and other local patriots, and the large sums of money they spent on legal proceedings, the Davie party were defeated in the end. From 1784 until 1835 the Fanes continued to rule Lyme Regis and take their seats in Parliament. It was not until the passing of the Reform Act of 1832 and the Municipal Reform Act of 1835 that justice was done and the power of the Fanes broken. In 1832 a constituency was formed that included both Lyme and Charmouth, which was represented in Parliament by only one member. From 1832 to 1842, and again from 1852 to 1865, the MP for Lyme and Charmouth was William Pinney of Somerton Erleigh in Somerset. The Fanes owned no property in Lyme and seldom entered the town. The inhabitants were treated with contempt by them, and one can imagine the great joy felt by all at the passing of the Municipal Reform Act. From that day the people of the town at last had a say in the management of their affairs.

This end to the days of political corruption was foreshadowed by the arrival in Lyme Regis of Edward John Gampier, one of the commissioners appointed to inquire into the state of corporations. A public inquiry was held in the Guildhall in Lyme on 13 and 14 December 1833. A full account of the proceedings before the commissioner was recorded by a local reporter. Charles Marr, the mayor, and George Smith, the town clerk, were firstly sworn in, and Mr Hillman, a solicitor, said he attended with a brief to watch proceedings. Smith, after specifying the bounds of the borough, went on to discuss the charters under which Lyme was governed. Later there was wide-ranging discussion of the constitution of the borough. Many of Smith's assertions seem open to question, but his evidence provides a valuable description of the way in which Lyme was governed, or misgoverned, in 1833.

During the course of the enquiry the actions of the corporation and its officials – the town clerk, recorder, chamberlain, coroner, Cobb-warden, etc. – came under review. Whenever money matters were being discussed, as they frequently were, the proceedings became noisy. The conduct of Peterson, the former chamberlain, generated much heat, and on one occasion the court had to be cleared. The chamberlain was the official responsible for the financial administration of the borough, including rents and Cobb dues. What appears to have been a glaring example of official negligence, misconduct and connivance was discussed at length. The offence involved the habitual removal of stones, piles and other building materials from the jetties, sea walls and The Cobb by burgesses, freemen and officials. The situation was aggravated by the failure of the corporation to maintain these in good repair, a responsibility laid fairly and squarely on their shoulders by an early charter. The mayor and town clerk tried to deny or minimize their responsibility, but Hillman gave himself the pleasure of reading out the relevant part of that charter.

Following the Reform Act of 1832, Lyme Regis was linked with Charmouth as a borough, to return only one MP, William Pinney. He represented Lyme from 1832 to 1842 and again from 1852 to 1865. He died in 1898 at the age of ninety-three

Lyme Regis in a painting of 1834, showing the old town

There was no doubt about their misconduct. Evidence of the offence included the fact that a jetty near the church had been dismantled and, as a result, both the churchyard and the church had suffered damage. It had been observed later that piles from the jetty had reappeared as gateposts at the house of Peterson, who was the chamberlain.

As for the neglect, it had been such as to induce Henry Holt Henley, lord of the manor, to bring an action against the corporation in 1826 on the grounds that the sea walls were defective and that his land had been flooded as a result. The case was tried at Dorchester. Henley succeeded and was awarded £100 damages. The corporation appealed time after time, but each time Henley won. In the end the case went to the House of Lords. The final judgment, given in 1834, was in Henley's favour and the corporation had to pay costs amounting to £3,041 10s., instead of a mere £100.

Many other matters were discussed, including the family relations of officials and members of the corporation, Cobb dues, charities and their funds, and the local school. The nature of the facts uncovered by the enquiry is indicated clearly by the report of the commission. This said, with remarkable restraint, that the commission had found the borough 'unimproved' and that all the members of the corporation seemed to be members of one family or to owe their position to the influence of that family.

CHAPTER THREE

The Mid-Victorians, 1841–70

Cyril Wanklyn, in his excellent book *Lyme Regis, a Retrospect*, gave a picture of how the town looked in the plan of 1841 and the changes that took place over the following twenty years. It was at this point that Lyme Regis moved decisively into nineteenth-century England, bringing to an end the old, essentially rural social system. To describe all of the changes in social habits and manners that have occurred since then would need a book much longer than this. For the middle classes and the rich the Victorian era was a happy age. Even the working classes had precise codes of behaviour and knew what to do on nearly every occasion that arose, in life and death.

In the mid-nineteenth century Lyme Regis was still primarily rural, with the inhabitants providing most of their own everyday needs. They built their own homes and made their own furnishings, the local mill and baker

Monmouth Street

The back beach on the east side of Gun Cliff, the preserve of the Curtis family

The beach in Victorian times

provided bread, and they grew their own fruit and vegetables. Many made their own clothes but, then as now, the ladies were interested in the latest fashions and would visit Mrs Bennett the straw-bonnet maker and her gentle daughter Maria. Twice a year the ladies of Lyme received an invitation to view the newest and most fashionable assortment of goods, which Mrs Bennett had just brought back from London to display in her shop in Church Street (now Malaba House). Ladies brought their straw hats to her to be cleaned (with oxalic acid) and trimmed, and gentlemen their panamas to be cleaned and reblocked.

The roads and streets of Victorian Lyme had a patina of dust and mud laced with horse droppings. The dirt must have trailed into many homes on skirt hems and shoes, causing much work for people like Mrs Lucas, the washerwoman. She lived beside the River Jordan, just beyond the lower Paradise Fields, and her hands and bare arms were shrivelled and white from always being in the soap suds. She always wore a white cap with a large frill round her face.

The needs of the local community were also served by people who travelled in from neighbouring farms and villages, many of them characters known far and wide. Mrs Hoare, the poultry woman, travelled in twice a week from Musbury with her donkey and panniers to sell chickens, ducks, eggs and vegetables. Mrs Bailey, the apple woman, drove her little donkey cart full of yellow apples around the town, and, as if from the constant contact, was as yellow, dry and shrivelled herself as any of the apples. Mr Henley, the chandler, also from Musbury, came in every week with his cart and boxes of candles. He was assisted by John Partridge, and the candles were made in four sizes, 8, 12, 14 and 16 to the pound. Milk and cream came into the town by horse and cart from farmers like Farmer Ruckley of Middle Mill Farm. His dairy, with its clean stone floor, had great square pans of scalded cream waiting for the next day's churn.

All of the shops in Lyme were privately owned, and the owner usually lived behind and over his shop. The shutters were taken down at 8.00 a.m. and the shop stayed open until 7.00 p.m. There was no midday break and no half day. Most of the shops were run by the family. Some took apprentices to learn the business. They were worked very hard and received little or no pay.

Credit was given to customers, and great deference was shown by the shopkeeper to the carriage trade. Those were the days when the customer was always right and nothing was too much trouble. People like Mrs Cannicott, the toy shop woman, and Mr Harvey, the grocer, greeted people with a politeness that would not be believed today.

One of the oldest shops trading in Lyme then was Penny the Drapers. This business was established in 1775 and its premises were at 23 Broad Street.

Broad Street from the top, with Thornton's the chemist (far left)

The first post office in Lyme Regis was in Norman House, which was in a section of Coombe Street, then known as Horse Street. In those days Lyme Regis had a postwoman called Mrs Boon. She was the wife of a local ironmonger, and she delivered the daily letters in a square, covered basket that she carried on her arm. The removal of this post office to Broad Street took place in 1853.

At this time the horse was supreme and gave employment to a large number of people in the town: wheelwrights and cartmakers, saddlers and blacksmiths, coachmen, stablemen and grooms, and firms that hired out both horses and vehicles. No self-respecting doctor with anything of a practice would walk on his rounds, and Dr Tucker, who lived in the Tudor House and was at the top of the medical profession in those days, rode a saddle-horse and drove his own dogcart.

One of the town's great characters was Gummer, generally known as Gummer the chairman. He used to hire himself out, together with three other men, two long poles and a true Sedan chair, with a roof that lifted and a glass door. He conveyed people to balls at The Assembly Rooms, musical parties and other gaieties. Gummer had a bald head, a few straggling locks of grey hair at his neck and acoss his forehead, and a red button of a nose. He always had a bright red handkerchief, which he constantly swept around his face and head. He was small and spare, and wore a long blue coat with brass buttons and a tall hat. In *Hunts Dorset Directory* of 1851 the name Nathaniel Booth, 'Sedan Chair Maker of Bridge Street', is given, but by that time this occupation had a limited future.

A contemporary of Gummer's was John Ham, a carpenter, who lived and had his workshop in Church Street. His workshop was opposite a farm threshing floor, in the days when farmworkers would thresh out the corn with flails. Another character was Fanny Frayle. She lived at 59 Silver Street and was known as 'Fanny the bathing woman'. She used to operate the ladies bathing machine. (The sexes were rigorously segregated when it came to bathing.) Fanny wore a wet blue petticoat, her good-tempered rosy face beaming out from inside her great sun-bonnet.

Law and order in the town were then in the capable hands of Bennett Wright, the constable, who paraded the streets keeping a watchful eye on everything. On Corporation Sundays (when the corporation went to church *en mass* for a special event) he walked to church with his stick, cocked hat and a blue frock-coat with gold buttons and much gold lace. He was envied by all who saw him and, known as a strict disciplinarian, was a terror to the local boys.

All Lymeites seem to have had titles then, such as Mr Roberts the schoolmaster, Miss Turle the schoolmistress, Jabez Wright the bootmaker and

Jericho Cottages, once known as Monkeys' Rough. The house at the rear was a mill and has now been converted into flats

The Fossil Depot with its whalebone outside. The building was demolished in 1913

Miss Anning the fossil woman. Fiddler Moore's son was known as Mr Moore the organist, who in turn had a son called Corelli, but who was known to all as Crawley Moore. Crawley had to leave Lyme in a hurry, having given information against a young man called Diamond, who had carried out a practical joke. Diamond was very popular, and Crawley would have received very rough treatment had he returned as Diamond had attempted suicide. Another local with a title was John Ham the pew opener. John, who wore black baggy trousers, a tailcoat and a white neckcloth, had a venerable appearance. He lived in Church Street in a cottage that was later occupied by Sam Curtis.

The old festivals and customs had not yet died away, and even for the poor there were days of pleasure and relaxation. One of the highlights of the year was the Michaelmas Fair, when Broad Street became the site for pens containing sheep, cattle and pigs. The sheep and cattle had an enclosure at the top of Broad Street while the pigs were near Bell Cliff. Great white cheeses were piled on the pavement in front of what is now Lloyds Bank, and a butter market was held in Church Street. The butter market must have presented a most attractive picture – the men in their elaborately worked white smocks and the women in various coloured-print sun-bonnets and aprons, all carrying big baskets full of butter and cream.

After the Michaelmas Fair was an Onion Festival, to which the men from the nearby village of Merriot brought their waggons loaded with onions and pickling cabbages. These were piled high in heaps on the pavement of Pyne House.

The Lyme Regis Gas and Range Company's works

Coram Court. The foundation stone of this building was laid in 1851

The Michaelmas Fair cheapjacks were in the street below Pyne House and then, as now, noisy crowds of young Lymeites swarmed around the stalls and shooting galleries. Very pretty pieces of crockery and ornaments could be bought there for a penny.

Regatta day was also a great time for celebration, and people came into the town from the surrounding countryside for the occasion. The day's events included racing, wrestling and rowing races for women. By 1855 it had become a day's holiday and, although much depended on the weather, it was a welcome break from the year's almost continuous hard work.

Bonfire night was another occasion for great excitement and much rough horseplay in the town. Guy Fawkes, of course, occupied the most prominent position and was paraded through the streets before being consigned to the flames.

On Christmas Eve a man called Jacky Fudge used to carry a lantern and lead the church choir from house to house singing carols. They would always finish with 'Mr and Mrs —— and all your family, we wish you a Happy Christmas and a Happy New Year'. On Christmas Eve, too, the mummers came and their pageant was usually held in the kitchen, with plenty of festive cheer.

The vicar was Parson Hodges, who conducted baptisms for the poor in the old baptistry during the afternoon service. Of course, the children of the rich were baptized as a special favour, not in public on a Sunday but on a week day. The point of interest in all baptisms was reached when the vicar kissed the baby with a kiss of peace, which he always did before he gave it back to the nurse or mother.

Dr Frederick Parry Hodges arrived in Lyme to become vicar in 1833. Born in 1800, he was a Dorset man and was related to the Fanes. When he first came to Lyme he stayed at Portland Cottage, but in 1851 the foundation stone of a new vicarage (now Coram Court) was laid, and he lived there until his death. He never married and was a much respected figure in Lyme. When the cemetery was first bought Frederick went to view it. 'This is a lovely place', he said. 'Yes sir', replied the Sexton, who was in attendance, 'and I have found the exact spot, sir, where I hope to have the pleasure of laying you.' Frederick remained vicar of Lyme until he died on 27 October 1880.

Mr Wayland was then the dissenting minister (Baptist). He had a most benevolent face, with long, flowing white hair that reached his shoulders. He was tall and thin, and always wore black kid gloves. Mr Wayland lived in Providence Place and had seven sons. The Baptist congregation began its separate existence at Lyme in 1653, with seventy-three members. It had previously been a branch of the parent congregation at Kilmington. The Baptist chapel was in Silver Street.

It was this era that brought one of the best-remembered visitors to the town, when Captain Maclure came to see one of the coastguards, who had sailed with him in the *Erebus* on an expedition to discover the North-west

This round tower was built in around 1830 to try a patent process for fulling cloth by steaming. The twin-gabled building in the background was once the Congregational chapel in Coombe Street and is now Dinosaurland

Passage. The people of Lyme threw a grand ball and supper for him in The Assembly Rooms.

Prominent citizens during this period included Robert Holmes, who was mayor in 1846, and Joseph Hayward. It was Hayward who took upon himself the entire prosecution of the lawsuit known as 'The Queen v. Ames', which was fought to establish the public right of way through Pinhay Cliffs.

Another leading family were the Warings, who were of Jewish descent. They originally lived in the Great House (now Boots) in Broad Street. The house had two very fine iron gates, with an eagle standing on each post, and a garden that ran down to the lower part of the town, which was called The Lynch.

In 1842 Henry Franks Waring built a house at the entrance of Stile Lane, on the site of the old bowling green. It was called South Cliff, and the foundation stone was laid by one-year-old Dolly Waring. Henry Waring was town clerk from 1836 to 1848. It was he who gave the name to Lucy's Jetty on the walk below South Cliff, where he used to moor a boat of that name.

Captain Charles Cocoper Benett, who lived at St Andrews, Clappentail Lane, was another wonderful character. He came to live in Lyme in 1821 after he retired from the Navy, and lived to the ripe old age of ninety-eight. His gardener and coachman was James Hallett, who was described as 'a very nice old-fashioned man'. He was the father of Selina Hallett, who won the mayor's competition for memories of Lyme Regis in July 1920. She was eighty-one when she wrote the prize-winning paper.

The entrance to the grounds of the Great House, Broad Street, Lyme Regis, *c.* 1860

Henry Franks Waring, who built South Cliff in 1842 and lived there for many years sitting by a window at South Cliff shortly before his death. Henry was the town clerk of Lyme from 1836 to 1848

During this period the quality of life improved for the middle class, old Lyme families and for the many newcomers to the town. There were musical evenings, card parties, balls, organized sports and many other entertainments. Mrs Cotton, assisted by her sister, Miss Gorton, organized parties for the children. Mrs Cotton later remarried and became Mrs Symonds. These parties were much enjoyed and, after playing games and dancing, the children had blancmange, jellies, macaroons, sponge cake and soft drinks before they were fetched by the family maid.

The middle classes were the great success story of the Victorian age. It was they who made the era what it was. The working classes lived very frugally and worked very hard. Prices were low but so also were their wages. Butcher's meat was only eaten on Sunday, but in mid-Victorian Lyme there was no real poverty, and everyone enjoyed a way of life with values and attitudes quite different from those of today.

CHAPTER FOUR

The Golden Age, 1870–1914

Between 1870 and the start of the First World War Lyme Regis enjoyed an increasing popularity as a seaside resort. Before 1871 most Victorians went to the beach only for their health, but the Bank Holiday Act of 1871 led to many social changes and gave seaside towns a new lease of life.

For the middle classes a holiday to Lyme required a great deal of preparation. The entire family would stay for as long as a month, and this would involve much packing of luggage. They would be accompanied by a maid and, in the case of younger families, a nanny as well.

When they arrived at the resort they found a variety of boarding houses and hotels to accommodate their needs. The premier hotel in the town was Hotel Alexandra, which opened in 1901. It was originally named Poullett House after the family who first owned it, and the last person to live there

Marine Parade, showing the cart road, *c.* 1870

Hotel Alexandra, 1911

The eastern part of Marine Parade, looking north from the foreshore, c. 1885

The entrance to Hotel Alexandra

before it became a hotel was the Revd Edward Peek. It was luxuriously furnished throughout and stood in five acres of grounds. The Three Cups Hotel in Broad Street was the oldest established hotel in the town, and in 1895 was under the personal supervision of the proprietress, a Mrs Garrod. There was a Three Cups Hotel at Lyme in the middle of the seventeenth century, but this was burned down in the great fire of 1844. The name derives from the arms of the Salters Company and may have been founded on the very early association of the borough with salt manufacture, which was the staple trade for centuries. The salt 'pans' (used to boil sea water for salt) and dues (tithes paid on the profits) belonged to the Abbott of Glastonbury. The Royal Lion Hotel was in Broad Street, too, and provided every comfort for families and commercial trade alike. A reading and smoking room for gentlemen and a ladies drawing-room were two of the many facilities.

Visitors to the town usually arrived by the Axminster–Lyme Regis horse bus, which was in operation by 1878. Two trips in each direction were made daily, and they connected at Axminster station with the most important trains to and from Waterloo. The owner of this service was John Groves of the Royal Lion Hotel, who died in July 1904. The drivers he employed included Tom Woodman, Harry Groves, and Harry and William Blake. The service closed down in 1903 with the opening of the new branch line. The

Silver Street, from outside Gravel Cottages, *c.* 1892. How quiet and peaceful it was then, with children deriving entertainment from games in the street

Broad Street, *c.* 1910. The Three Cups Hotel (right) advertised 'Good stabling', but the AA sign (front of hotel) shows that they were already catering for motorists

Axminster and Lyme Regis Light Railway opened on Monday 23 August of that year.

The other well-known service was the Lyme–Charmouth–Bridport horse bus with the famous coach *Defiance*. This departed from The Three Cups Hotel, and William Hounsell, who drove the coach from 1880 to 1901, was considered to be one of the best four-in-hand drivers in the south-west. In the years before 1914 the new railway was a great success, and by 1910 sixty thousand passengers were travelling between Axminster and Lyme annually, thus bringing prosperity to the seaside town.

The *Lyme Regis Mirror*, which was published every Saturday morning, priced 1d., carried a list of the visitors and where they were staying. It was very important to be included on this list, which must have served as a local *Who's Who*.

The resort had many simple delights to please old and young alike. These included fishing trips with wonderful local characters such as Joe Curtis, who lived on Church Cliffs and was one of a large family of boatmen and fishermen. During the summer months visitors could take sea trips on Cosen's and Co. Steamers from Weymouth, visiting places such as Sidmouth, Torquay, Dartmouth and Weymouth, and enjoying the special views of the Dorset and Devon coastline.

Then, as now, people on holiday were eager to have a keepsake to remind them of their visit, and it was during this period that the souvenir industry

Victoria Hotel, *c.* 1907. This was the nearest hotel to the railway station and stood 250 feet above sea level

Marine Parade, c. 1910

Buddle Bridge, looking seaward from the north side, 1921

entered a new phase. Holiday-makers often paid a visit to Darby's, a china, glass, fine art and gift shop at 8 Broad Street, to purchase plates, ashtrays, cups and dishes inscribed and decorated with the borough of Lyme Regis arms and seal. Another popular gift to take home for friends was the crested china popularized by W.H. Goss, which included items such as paddle-steamers, bathing huts and fishermen's baskets.

This was also the dawn of the golden age of the postcard. Plain postcards appeared in 1870, and by 1880 the first of those bearing pictures began to appear. Everyone on holiday sent cards back home, and today the seaside postcard has a special place in the collector's heart.

Although the appearance of Broad Street has not greatly changed, the old names over the shops have disappeared and the Dorset dialect is seldom heard. Much of the rich local character has gone, and we are poorer for that. Broad Street had traders such as A.M. Burge, a family grocer and tea dealer, who also sold wines and spirits. His shop was the only thatched property in Broad Street. It still sells wine and spirits but now belongs to Victoria Wines. James Farnham, another well-known character, was a jeweller and watchmaker, and also made fossil jewellery. This is still a thriving local craft, indeed fossils have become a major industry in present-day Lyme. Bert Lane's shop was at 22

Broad Street, *c.* 1889

Broad Street, a site now occupied by the National Westminster Bank, and it was well patronized by residents and visitors alike. Even on informal occasions costume for the middle class was rigid and inflexible, and Lane provided all of the new season's goods in the latest styles. The shop also kept a variety of gentlemen's shooting and golfing boots. Ladies' and gent's boots and shoes were sold by P. Booth, who traded in Broad Street. Booth advertised 'repairs of every description neatly and expeditiously executed'.

Fashionable Lyme would also pay a visit to Penny and Co. in the shop at 23 Broad Street. Victorian women pursued elegance in their clothes, sacrificing comfort and subjecting their bodies to the rigid confinement of tightly laced corsets. Penny's, as well as providing wedding outfits, family mourning clothes, dresses, furs and silks, also sold tight-lacing corsets with wonderful names, such as Browns Dermathistic and The Y & N Patent Diagonal Seam.

Mr Sam Harris, the butcher, traded from 65 Broad Street and also had a slaughterhouse in the vicinity of the Guildhall. He called on local families daily for orders and described himself as a 'purveyor of choice English meat'.

Smith's Restaurant, Broad Street, *c.* 1913

Looking down Church Street, *c.* 1912

The meat fragments left over after he had carved up the joints were always sold on Saturday nights, and for many families were the only meat they tasted.

George Henley, the chemist, occupied 45 Broad Street. His patent medicine, at 1s. a bottle, must have been a remarkable bargain, for it was advertised as a cure for colds, coughs, bronchitis, influenza, all weakness and ailments of the chest and lungs. His shop was once a part of the site known as the Great House. It was here, in the summer of 1773, that William Pitt (1728–78), First Earl of Chatham and War Minister of George II, stayed from 6 June until 28 September with his son, the great William Pitt (1759–1806), Prime Minister of George III.

John Beer, the local hairdresser, also lived in Broad Street. His small house, once occupied by Mary Anning and her mother, was described as a place with hardly enough room to turn around. Here, however, this much loved local character successfully raised a family of four daughters and two sons. The shop and house were later to become a part of Haddon's shop.

Church Street was the home of Mr F.W. Shephard. His photographic studio was at No. 57, and the people of Lyme were attracted to his premises by an ever-changing display of photographs showing local people and events. Shephard described himself as a landscape and portrait photographer. He also provided a darkroom for the use of amateurs.

Next door to Mr Shephard lived Mr Huxford, who was the local goods agent and the carrier for the L&SW Railway. All this was carried out with his

Opening day of Lyme Regis railway, 24 August 1903

Lyme Regis railway station, c. 1907

two-horse dray, driven by Mr Frank Mitchell. Before the Lyme branch railway Mr Huxford carried all goods to Lyme from Axminster station. Church Street was also the home of Sergeant-major Britton of the Lyme Company of the Royal Artillery Volunteers. His wife kept a general stores at the Guildhall corner, by the entrance to the drill hall.

The first cycle shop in Lyme was in Church Street and belonged to Mr Hallett. He also repaired umbrellas, and his shop sign was an umbrella fixed on the wall above the shop door. The business ceased when the premises were burned down.

At the end of Church Street was a farmhouse with outbuildings and a rick yard (for hayricks), where Farmer Woodman lived. His two daughters helped him, doing a local milk round on foot and measuring out the milk at customers' doors from a two gallon can. Local children flocked to the farmyard at threshing time, when Buglers travelling steam engine for threshing came for a week's work.

The first of the royal celebrations during this period took place in 1887. Early in that year public attention was concentrated on the approaching Golden Jubilee of the queen's reign. There was a rare outburst of loyal devotion and gratitude, and the proposal to make 21 June the Jubilee Day met with general approval. The day in Lyme was brilliantly fine, every street was gay with bunting and a programme of events was enjoyed by all. To commemorate the queen's Jubilee the Revd E. Peek, at his own expense, restored the interior of the Guildhall, while the corporation, out of the revenue of the borough, rebuilt the exterior. It was during this year that Zachary Edwards, one of Lyme's most respected gentlemen, was mayor of the borough.

A cottage hospital containing eight beds was established in 1875. To celebrate the Diamond Jubilee of 1897 the Jubilee Cottage Hospital was

The Roman Catholic church

The Old Mill, 1901

Buddle Bridge during the widening of Bridge Street, looking east and showing the southern walls of the Priests' Chamber, which had been opened up during the widening work, 1913. In the wall is a recess with a stone arch, the so-called Aumbrey

established in Church Street at a cost of £900. The first matron was Miss Coombes, who did much good work in the formative years. She was succeeded by Miss Owen. The site in Church Street later became inadequate and the hospital moved to Herne Lee, a house in Pound Road. This property was given by the Revd G. Eyre in memory of his mother, who lived there for some years.

The Victorian era ended on the evening of 22 January 1901, when the people of Lyme heard that Queen Victoria, surrounded by her children and grandchildren, had died. It was the beginning of a new century, with many improvements taking place. In Coombe Street the Marder almshouses, a new erection of eight tenements for old seamen, had just been completed at a a cost of £2,000, the money having come from a bequest in the will of Captain Nicholas Marder. Langmoor Gardens, facing the sea front on rising ground, was given to the town in 1913 by James Moly of Langmoor Manor. Although the town had long been illuminated by gaslight, the number of street lamps had been increased. The gas works had been enlarged and the gas company had acquired a new office in Poole's Court, where fires and cookers could be bought.

By 1914 the leisure facilities for the working classes were greatly increased and improved, giving the people of Lyme more varied opportunities for amusement. However, 1914 was also the end of a golden summer.

Marine Parade, *c.* 1907

The threat of war that had been hanging over Europe reached a climax on 4 August, when Sir Edward Grey, the Minister of Foreign Affairs, stood up in the House of Commons and declared war against Germany. For the first time since Napoleon, war became more than an adventure in foreign parts. Much excitement was felt by the people in Lyme, since local men were serving in the Navy, the Army and also the Reserves. War fever swept the town, but few then realized that this war would last four long years, and that the devastation and slaughter would be impossible to imagine.

Torpedo flotilla and submarines off Lyme Regis, 24 July 1908

CHAPTER FIVE

The Twentieth Century, 1914–65

During the first days of the First World War there was a steady enrolment of men from Lyme Regis. The first Sunday after the declaration of war, 9 August 1914, was set apart as a day of intercession for divine mercy and the safety of the Empire. The parish church of St Michael's was crowded, and the impressive service closed with the singing of the National Anthem. It was at this service that Lyme Regis men of military age were urged to fight for England, and many responded to the call.

The war years were a time of great hardship and sadness, and local people, with their minds full of danger, saw suspicious meanings in everything.

The Bay Hotel, Marine Parade, *c.* 1934. This hotel was built in 1924, and at that time advertised inclusive summer terms from £5 5s. a week

Marine Parade, *c.* 1921. The twin chimneys of the old cement works are in the background

Rumours swept the town: it was reported to Scotland Yard that a German submarine base had been established in Pinhay Bay; and a man picking limpets on the beach was reported on the grounds that he was sending messages to U-boats.

By 1918 there were severe shortages of food. It seemed as if the war would never end, and news from the front was anxiously awaited. Light relief was

Marine Parade

Jericho, *c.* 1921

Colway Lane, *c.* 1919

provided when, on a cold February afternoon in 1918, a seaplane 2 to 3 miles from shore was observed to collapse suddenly and fall straight into the water. The lifeboat call was immediately sounded and a crew was assembled with difficulty, as most of the lifeboat members were on National Service. The tide was very low and the crew had much trouble moving the boat through the mud, but it was finally launched amid ironic cheers from the spectators. In the meantime motor trawlers had arrived on the scene and rescued the pilot, and were able to tow the plane to Beer.

The 'war to end all wars' ended on 11 November 1918. The townspeople gathered in Broad Street to celebrate restored peace, and flags were hung from all shop windows. Of those men who had gone from Lyme Regis, there were many who did not return, and those that did found a changed England, with signs that the insular life of Lyme Regis was ebbing to its close.

After the end of the Great War the old social order was a mere shadow of its former self and the people of Lyme Regis moved into the 'gay twenties' with new attitudes. Pre-1914 days had no charms for the young, particularly the young women – they had broken away and were not going back.

It was during the 1920s that the motorist and the motor car came into their own, with local garages such as Owens of Coombe Street catering for their needs. Owens were also the proprietors of the All White motor coaches, and, judging by their advertisements, were firm believers in 'small is beautiful'. They described their coaches as 'small and safe, with no coach more than a 14-seater and all fitted with 4 wheel brakes'. F.B. Watson had a garage in Broad Street and was the official repairer for the AA. He owned the

Blue Bird motor coaches and also sold petrol from the pump, which was quite an innovation.

Excitement was high in the town on 27 December 1922, when competitors in the Motor Cycle Club's Boxing Night Trial passed through Lyme on the return journey from Exeter to London. Motor cycles taking part included Super Chief Indians with 10 hp engines, and cars such as GNs, Rovers, Bentleys, 50 hp Napiers and even a Rolls Royce. The Rolls, with its all-weather body fitted and electric lamps burning inside, looked to be the height of comfort.

It was during this time that the Philpot Museum opened and the first curator, Dr Wyatt Wingrave, opened a gallery in the museum devoted to a display of representative fossils. Then, as now, the fossils of Lyme Regis were world-famous, and there was not a museum of importance that did not possess one of Lyme's palaeontological treasures.

It was in the 1920s that the first regular cinema opened, providing local people with additional entertainment. By all accounts a drink at the 'local' was still a much-favoured pastime. Indeed, at the licensing sessions in February 1929 a petition signed by fifty-two people wished to draw attention to the fact that 'the number of places in this town where alcoholic refreshment may be obtained, when compared with the population, remains the very highest in the Kingdom'. The authorities were urged to grant no fresh facilities and to reduce the number of those already in existence.

St Michael's Hotel, *c.* 1921

Lyme Regis County Secondary School, Woodman Road, *c.* 1925

Typical of the times was that the builders A. & F. Wiscombe, who had premises in Broad Street, were advertising building sites for houses and bungalows. It was during the inter-war period that the building trade boomed, and by 1939 a third of all of the houses in Britain had been built during the previous twenty years.

The National Town Criers' Championship was held in the grounds of Colway, Lyme Regis, on 18 August 1932, when W. Abbot, the Lyme crier,

The County Secondary School from the playing field, *c.* 1929. The headmaster at this time was Mr A.W.M. Greenfield MA (Oxon)

The junction of Coombe Street and Bridge Street, looking west from the museum

Madeira Cottage, 1929. Notice the bow windows and the porches of lattice work – veritable suntraps. Little Madeira was added in 1935

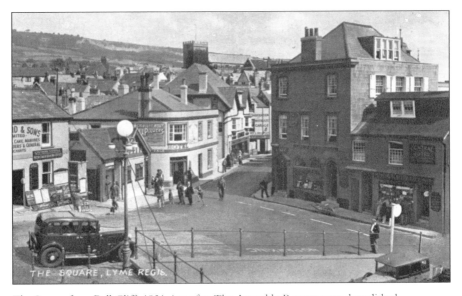

The Square from Bell Cliff, 1931, just after The Assembly Rooms were demolished

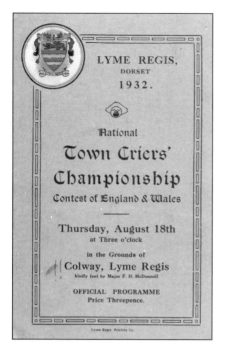

Official programme of the Town Criers'
Championship, 1932

retained his title against twenty-two contenders. Mr Abbott won the
championship at Great Torrington in 1930 and again at Lyme in 1931. He
was the Sarjeant at Mace and Mayor's Officer, and his office dated back to the
year 1200. His crier's robes dated back to the sixteenth century, and his silver
badge of office was made in Exeter in 1710. In 1932 Mr Abbott completed
thirty-seven years of service in the local lifeboat crew.

The Silver Jubilee of George V, followed by his death in 1936, led up to
the coronation celebrations of George VI on 21 May 1937. Lyme
celebrated in style, beginning with a parade from the Town Hall, with the
British Legion, Guides, Scouts and many other local organizations, to a
United Service in Langmoor Gardens. This was followed by a dinner for a
hundred old people, then sports on the sands and tea for the children. The
highlight of the day was the opening of the new full-size bowling green
near The Cobb.

In July 1939 foreign boats were still carrying cargoes of timber to Lyme.
During this month a German motor vessel, the *Dietrich Hasseldieck*, entered
the harbour to discharge part of a cargo of timber of 104 tons. The ship had
come from Blankaholm, a port in Sweden, and left Lyme for West Bay. That
same week the British vessel *Hanna* discharged 150 tons of cement, which she
had brought from the Isle of Man. All this was to change when the people of

The Holiday Fellowship at Coram Court, 14 September 1931

Marine Parade, looking west, *c.* 1926

Umbrella cottage, 1937

Lyme heard Mr Chamberlain speaking over the radio saying, in a strained voice, that we were at war with Germany.

A few days after the outbreak of the Second World War, building workers saw a plane circling above as if it was seeking bearings, then the engine of the plane spluttered and the aircraft dived nose-first into the ground. There was suspicion of spying, but the monoplane belonged to a company director from Exmouth, Mr Henry Foulds. The plane crashed into a field near the Seaton–Lyme Regis main road and the pilot was killed instantly.

During the early months of the war the Air Council obtained consent from the Board of Trade for the use of an area of tidal lands in Lyme Bay, about 8 miles seaward of Lyme Regis, for explosives practice. Bombs were not to exceed 120 lb in weight unless they were filled with sand. The local fishermen were given assurance that a patrol boat would be present during bombing to ensure their safety.

In the autumn of 1941 the gallery on the ground floor of the museum was requisitioned for the ARP Control Centre and was not returned until the spring of 1946.

When Germany surrendered in May 1945 there was general rejoicing. However, during the post-war years great social change took place and much of the old character of Lyme Regis disappeared for ever. In August 1955 the Housing Committee agreed to build more council houses owing to the length of the waiting list. At the meeting Councillor Mrs Staples asked why a man, who had left his employment in the town, had been allocated a house

Lyme Bantams, 1930/31 team, who were the Perry Street League Intermediate Champions. Back row, left to right: Wiggy Boalch, -?-, -?-, Cuthbert Powell, Fred Perry, -?-. Front row: Bill Ryder, ? Curtiss, Bob Dunne, Cecil Searle, ? Collier.

Cup winners, Lyme Regis, 1930s

Football Cup celebrations, Lyme Regis, 1930s

Lyme Football Club, *c.* 1951. Back row, left to right: –?–, Bert Trueman, Bob Wheeler, Jack Loveridge, John Loder, –?–, Alan Wellman, John Perry, Clive Enticott, Tommy Perryn, Alderman King (mayor), Alderman Jack Bowditch. Front row: Jack Potter, Fred Smith, Cecil Hodges, Henry Broom, –?–, Bill Wood, Pete Loveridge, Bob Mason

Lyme Regis Home Guard

The end of Marine Parade with the Royal Standard on the left, September 1948

when local people badly in need were unable to secure one. Councillor E.J. Hallett said this was not the first time this had occurred, and that they had even found that one person working in Wales and another in Canada were on the list.

There was much excitement in 1959 when, that June, hundreds of holiday-makers saw The Spindles, a picturesque thatched house in Hay Lane, owned by Mr J. Awford, destroyed by fire. The lawn looked like a jumble sale as neighbours, holiday-makers and boys from Lyme Regis Grammar School helped to save the furniture and other possessions. National news was made in August 1960, when the brakes failed on a lorry carrying a party of boy scouts down Broad Street. The vehicle veered from side to side as the driver tried desperately to find a heavy enough obstruction to halt it. The lorry finally stopped when it collided with a railway van, but in its wake it left a trail of destruction: a smashed shop front, broken lamp standards, and mangled cars and commercial vehicles. None of the scouts in the lorry was seriously hurt, but many pedestrians were injured and a three-year-old child and a woman of seventy were killed.

Today Lyme Regis continues as a busy, thriving town. Over the years it has undergone many changes, but it has been able to adapt to the changing requirements without losing too much of its character. Changes of occupation and retirement have brought into the town a large population who were not born there. Incomers now outnumber the true natives, but hopefully all will help to preserve the rich inheritance that has been handed down through the generations.

CHAPTER SIX

Triumphs and Disasters

THE SIEGE OF LYME, 1644

During the Civil War the inhabitants held Lyme for Parliament against the king, successfully resisting the siege of the town and finally compelling Prince Maurice to retire in disgrace from their defences. The attack began on 20 April 1644 and continued until 15 June, when the Earl of Essex came to the rescue.

The town defences consisted of a dry ditch, a few earthworks thrown up in haste and three small batteries: Davies Fort, standing a little above Church Cliffs on a high mound looking towards Uplyme, Gun Cliff and the fort at Cobb Gate, the latter two being small batteries on the seashore, covering the bay.

The king's troops were concentrated around Colway and Hay, and totalled four thousand men. Prince Maurice was confident that he could subdue the town and restore it to his uncle, Charles I, but he had reckoned without the presence in Lyme of a 'thick-set man in early middle life, of a low stature; however, of a quick, lively eye and of a good soldier-like countenance; a man of singularly modest and noble expression, a born leader of his fellows'. Although the garrison at Lyme came under Colonel Ceely, he wisely gave a free hand to this man, his second-in-command, Robert Blake, who came from Bridgwater. Blake was stern, blunt and courageous, and was later to become the Lord Admiral of the Fleet. His well-planned leadership inspired the people of Lyme in their heroic defence.

When the prince came down from the hills of Somerset, Blake counted his forces and found that the number did not exceed five hundred men. The town, though its spirit was good, afforded little aid, for its whole population fell short of a thousand souls. Yet for eight weeks the fine army of the Royalists was baffled by an enemy with a handful of men and mudworks for ramparts.

There is no doubt that the women of Lyme were as brave as the men, and took a very active part in the defence of their town. One of them is reported to have fired off her musket more than sixteen times in resistance of one assault. Another, who had already had a hand cut off, declared that she would sacrifice the other, and even her life, rather than yield.

The men lost by the cavaliers amounted to two thousand, more than had fallen in the conquests of Exeter and Bristol. The garrison had to mourn the loss, among others, of Captain Pyne, who was mortally wounded on 22 May. On Sunday 16 June a service of thanksgiving was held. The preacher was no less a man than the celebrated Hugh Peters, who was acting then as chaplain to the Earl of Warwick.

THE MONMOUTH LANDING, 1685

The landing of the misguided Duke of Monmouth and his followers at Lyme Regis in June 1685 was the last great historical event in connection with the town. The duke came ashore via the beach west of The Cobb. Once he had landed he knelt on the shore and thanked God for having preserved the friends of liberty and pure religion from the perils of the sea and asked the blessing of heaven to rest on his enterprise. This was a moment of great excitement and Monmouth, who was dressed in purple with a star on his breast, entered the town and set up his banner in the market-place. His declaration of purpose was read from the market cross. As soon as his identity was known, crowds of spectators cried 'A Monmouth, a Monmouth. The Protestant religion.' Monmouth's crusade, which was of a semi-theological character, came to a disastrous end at Sedgemoor. It cost the town a large number of lives for, in addition to those killed in battle and those transported, twelve who had enlisted in his army were executed on the spot where he had landed. They were not all men from Lyme, but in the eyes of Judge Jeffreys that mattered little.

James II was bent on a terrible revenge, and the behaviour of his lord chief justice when he conducted the Bloody Assizes was beyond anything heard of in a civilized nation. Lyme suffered severely and had to pay dearly for its outburst of Protestant enthusiasm. Its inhabitants had ample reason for regretting their ready and generous aid to such an ill-fated rebellion.

LIGHTNING STRIKE, 1800

A group of horsemen gave a series of displays in a field near Lyme, showing off their riding skills. The show proved to be very popular and attracted large crowds. One afternoon Mary Anning, then fifteen months old, was taken to the display by her nurse, Elizabeth Haskins, who carried her in her arms. Unfortunately it began to rain hard, so the crowd began to disperse. Some quickly left the field, while others took shelter in the hedges and under a

The Duke of Monmouth in hunting dress

Sightseers from Lyme Regis viewing the burning 'volcano', which happened in 1908 about half a mile east of the town and was caused by the combustion of pyrites

group of elm trees. Suddenly there was a deafening clap of thunder and a vivid flash of lightning, after which a group of figures was seen lying motionless under one of the trees. People rushed to the scene and found that Elizabeth Haskins and two fifteen-year-old girls had been killed by the lightning. Mary Anning appeared to be dead, but revived after being placed in a bath of warm water. It was said that before this event Mary had been a dull, weak and sickly child, but her health improved immediately and she grew up to be a lively and intelligent girl.

THE LANDSLIP, 1839

Owing to the nature of the geology, the cliffs between Lyme Regis and Beer have always been prone to landslips. Records show that since the sixteenth century there have been many minor slips and at least five larger ones. The cliffs are made up of three distinct layers, the lowest layer being gault, covered by greensand, with chalk on the top. Rain is able to penetrate the porous chalk but not the impervious clay. In a very wet season, therefore, the intermediate greensand becomes saturated and converted to a mass of quicksand. The bedding in the cliffs dips slightly towards the sea, so, with the quicksand acting as a lubricant, sections of the heavy, saturated chalk tend to slip downwards.

The largest and most spectacular slip occurred at Dowlands, below Bindon Manor, at Christmas 1839 after a very wet autumn. Nearly 35 acres of land subsided from the cliff, creating a vast chasm half a mile long. A large section,

The Landslip, *c.* 1885

about 15 acres, remained intact, still with its hedges and growing corn, and this is now known as Goat Island.

The event was fully recorded at the time by the Revd W.D. Conybeare, the vicar of Axminster, who was an eminent geologist. He says that cracks had been opening in the ground throughout the previous week, but as this often happened in the area it did not cause undue concern.

On Christmas Eve two labourers from Dowland Farm went to the farm for their traditional Ashen Faggot supper. Their cottages were low on the cliff, and on their return they noticed that there had been more subsidence during the day. They went home to bed but were woken at 4.00 a.m. The walls of their cottages were 'rending and sinking', and they saw fissures opening in the ground around them. At 6.00 a.m. they went to warn Mr Chappel, the farmer, but found that their path was almost cut off since there had been a fresh subsidence of several feet since midnight. One of the cottages was completely ruined and the other was badly cracked and damaged.

Cracks continued to open all day on 25 December, and there were several considerable subsidences. The main slip took place that night, when two coastguards on watch at around midnight saw the start of the fissures that created the great chasm. Cracks began to open all around, and the men heard noises that they described as 'like the rending of cloth'.

At the same time that the cliff was slipping a reef was raised from the seabed, about three-quarters of a mile in length. Two other coastguards on Culverhole Beach that night witnessed the elevation of this submarine reef, which rose to a height of about forty feet.

Throughout 26 December the chasm continued to sink and the reef to rise, but by the end of the day the worst was over. The reef was later gradually dispersed by wave action. There was a further large slip at Whitlands in February 1840, and there are still minor slippages almost every year.

The event caused great excitement and thousands of people came from miles around to view the devastation. There was even a dance called the Landslip Quadrille, which was popular in London. The following August the corn, which had continued to grow on the slipped section, was harvested. A great fête was held to mark the occasion, booths were erected and bands played. The reapers were led by a party of young ladies, dressed as the Nymphs of Ceres. The landslip at Lyme is the largest and most important example on the coast of Great Britain, and since 1955 it has been designated a National Nature Reserve. The area contains interesting birds, butterflies and flora, and continues to attract many visitors.

THE FIRE, 1844

The crowded centre of Lyme Regis was ravaged by two fires early in the nineteenth century. The first, in 1803, was the less disastrous, although a

This drawing of the fire at Lyme Regis on 11 May 1844 is reproduced from the *Illustrated London News* edition of 18 May of that year

Dunster print of The Square from Bell Cliff, *c.* 1840. The building on the left is the old Three Cups Hotel, which was burned down in the 1844 fire

Lyme Regis Fire Brigade, 1908. Mr Foxwell (seated second from left) was the captain

contemporary report says 'the fire-engines, of which there were three, do not appear to have been in such repair as to be used with any considerable effect'.

The 1844 fire was altogether more serious. Although one report says that the fire started in a baker's shop, it does seem to have started at The George, which was an enormous hostelry, famous from medieval times. The inn stood on the land between Coombe Street, Church Street and Monmouth Street, and anyone of note who visited Lyme would have stayed there. The room where Monmouth slept was displayed to visitors right up to the time of the fire. This establishment had gone downhill with the general decline in prosperity in Lyme after 1750, and to a certain extent its pre-eminent place had been taken by the smaller Three Cups Hotel.

On the morning of 11 May, following two months of drought, a strong north-east wind was blowing. The fire raged from 10.00 a.m. to 10.00 p.m, and soon affected Coombe Street, Bridge Street and the bottom end of Broad Street. Both The Three Cups and The George were destroyed. The old Market Place was soon engulfed, with The Customs House and the old Shambles. The loss of The Shambles may not have been considered to be such a bad thing, but Mary Anning wrote at the time, 'I do regret the old clock that had stood for centuries'. Fifty houses were wholly or partly burned out and the owners made homeless.

A public meeting was held to assess the needs of those affected and a committee was formed. It raised over £450, which was distributed as relief. The Three Cups moved at once to the premises occupied by Hiscotts Boarding House. The centre of Lyme was rebuilt as quickly as possible, the old Market and shops were redeveloped and a new customs house was built at the bottom of Cobb Road. Many historic buildings, including The George and The Market Place, were lost and the face of Lyme was changed for ever.

THE WRECK OF THE *HEROINE*, 1852

A day long remembered by the people of Lyme is 27 December 1852, when a vessel named the *Heroine* got into difficulties near Beer Head. She was a boat bound for Australia, carrying thirty-eight people – men, women and children – thirty of them being emigrants. The ship was large and was driven inshore on a dangerous coast by adverse winds. Lying four miles offshore, she fired distress signals every five minutes. Lyme had no lifeboat. Five brave men came forward and put out from The Cobb in the revenue cutter. Lifebuoys were brought and positioned in the long white boat, and, amid cheers from the crowd, the men set out on their rescue attempt. At the moment they left The Cobb the enormous waves overturned the boat, and four of the men were drowned in sight of the town. The bodies of the four men were

The launching of the *Susan Ashley* lifeboat

covered, a Union Jack placed over them and they were carried to The Pilot Boat Inn, a temporary mortuary, to await a funeral with full honours. The men of Lyme have a long history of service and then, as now, were prepared to give all to help their fellow men.

Ironically the rescue attempt need not have taken place. Later on two lifeboats from the *Heroine*, containing all of the passengers, drifted in below Church Cliffs. The only casualty was the captain. He was the last to leave his boat and, in doing so, he broke his leg. When the good people of Lyme discovered that most of the emigrants were not only shipwrecked, but also destitute, they decided to raise a fund. A meeting was held in the town hall to make the distribution.

Whit Sunday Flood, 1890

The morning of Whit Sunday 1890 was bright with sunshine and the heat was oppressive. Just after 2.00 p.m. thunder was heard in the distance and black clouds were seen rising over Portland Bill. Soon the sky was dark with inky clouds and people came out into the street, attracted by the blackness of the sky and the noise of the thunder.

The centre of the storm circled Lyme and the rain poured down in torrents for more than three hours. This caused a flood, which rushed down the valley to Lyme, uprooting trees, sweeping away the river banks and walls, and washing away wooden footbridges, leaving them hanging in the trees by the riverside. The top part of a bridge at Mill Green was swept away and the water came down to the back of the mill, breaking through the high garden wall of Temple House, through the boundary wall and into Coombe Street. Houses were flooded, and in some places people were rescued from their bedroom windows by men in boats. The roads were washed out in great holes, and for weeks following the storm people came from miles away to view the destruction. A charitable fund to help the distressed was raised by the mayor, Zachary Edwards.

LOSS OF HMS *FORMIDABLE*, 1 JANUARY 1915

HMS *Formidable* was a pre-war Dreadnought battleship that carried a complement of 790 officers and men. On 1 January 1915 it was struck by a torpedo at about 1.30 a.m., some miles off the Devon coast. It sank an hour and a half afterwards. Owing to the rough sea and intense cold there were only about two hundred survivors.

One of the ship's cutters grounded on the beach in front of Marine Parade in Lyme Regis. This boat contained fifty-seven men, of whom six were dead and three more died on the beach. The boat had been in the sea for over twenty hours and the men in her took off their boots so as to use them to bail out the water.

The Pilot Boat Hotel, Bridge Street, *c*. 1918

The survivors were taken to The Pilot Boat Hotel where blankets and warm clothes were provided by the people of Lyme. After they had revived, the local people took them into their own homes and gave them food.

The funeral of six of the men took place at Lyme Regis five days later, with the Bishop of Salisbury officiating. The parish church was full for the ceremony, with all the streets on the funeral route lined with people paying their respects.

LYME TO CHARMOUTH ROAD SLIP, 1928

In 1826 a new road was built between Lyme Regis and Charmouth. The previous road had been up a very steep hill and, according to a contemporary report, 'in mercy to postmasters, pedestrians and quadrupeds, a less ambitious access to the ancient Port of Lyme was projected'. The road ran for two miles, mostly parallel to the curve of the bay, and on the precipitous side the land sloped gently down for about 250 feet to the beach below. Railings were placed along this edge, and the panoramic vista of Lyme and the whole bay was almost unrivalled.

In the space of three winters, however, the road was almost ruined. Undermined by springs, the foundations were gradually swept away, and after a very wet season a whole mass sank in January 1828. The drop was to a depth of eight feet at one end and twenty at the other, in a smooth curve. The hollow beneath was so complete that there were no undulations on the crown of the road; even the railings preserved their relative position.

Charmouth Cutting. This is the old Charmouth coast road that slipped away in 1928

The road was rebuilt, but history repeated itself exactly a hundred years later. The road had been closed to vehicles for a couple of years owing to earlier minor falls, but on 30 January 1928 there was an appreciable subsidence. Once again there was a drop of twenty feet at the western end, and this time the road had to be closed completely.

THE WRECK OF THE *ST MICHEL*, 1937

A group of local boys became heroes overnight when they rescued the crew of a French cargo vessel that ran aground between Lyme and Charmouth in January 1937. The 150 ton *St Michel* had lost its sails in a gale and had to rely on a small auxiliary engine, which was of little use in the mountainous seas. The crew anchored the boat off Lyme Regis, but she dragged her anchor and ran aground. Charlie Hallett, an errand boy, was at the cinema when the boat sent out distress signals. He ran to his home at the top of the cliff, donned Wellington boots and scrambled down to the beach. He was joined by a group of local Rovers and Boy Scouts. As he knew the paths so well Hallett was the first down, and he saw a member of the French crew trying to climb to safety. The man spoke no English, but signalled that he would not leave without the rest of the crew. A search was made, and the three other men were found. They were making frantic efforts to climb the cliff, but the surface was too slippery. Hallett said that he had never been in such a mess. Normally there were bogs, but this time almost the whole of the cliff was a quagmire. On two occasions his boots were wrenched from his feet by the clinging mud. Once he sank more than two feet into a bog but was pulled out by one of the Rovers.

Many people were waiting at the cliff top to help with the final ascent. The crew were taken to The Pilot Boat Hotel, where they were given dry clothes and a bed for the night. A local resident said that there had been many subsidences on this part of the cliff, which made it dangerous to climb even in daylight. On such a night it was very plucky of Hallett and the Scouts to risk so much.

There had been controversy a few years earlier when *The Thomas Masterman Hardy*, the Lyme Regis lifeboat, had been withdrawn. A local resident said that, as there had now been five wrecks since the boat had been removed, there was sufficient cause for strong representations to be made for its reinstatement.

LISTER GARDENS SLIP, 1962

Lyme Regis has a long history of land instability, the most vulnerable area being the slopes behind Marine Parade. In the 1920s small slips often occurred in Langmoor Gardens, until the debris finally caused the collapse of the retaining wall and slipped onto the beach. Later there were more slips in

Landslip in Langmoor Gardens, *c.* 1926

the area of Cliff House, which caused cracks to develop in Cobb Road, and in 1951 a retaining wall was built to try to support the road. By this time two houses in Cobb Road had been damaged so badly that they had to be demolished.

In 1961 preparation work was begun for the building of some twenty houses on the slope below Cliff House. Owing to the history of slipping it was decided to remove a large amount of material from the site, so as to produce a much gentler gradient, and to install additional deep drainage. Lyme Regis Borough Council were in favour of this action, and around 20,000 cubic metres of material were removed during the winter of 1961/2. However, a few days after the work had been completed, it was noticed that the ground in Lister Gardens was cracking and moving. On 12 February 1962 the whole slope gave way spectacularly – an area of about 200 metres by 100 metres slipped several metres in only a minute. Cliff House moved more than three metres towards the sea and later had to be demolished, and Cliff Cottage tilted and was badly damaged. The plans to build the twenty houses were abandoned and the land was used instead for public gardens.

CHAPTER SEVEN

Personalities

Lyme Regis has produced a number of notable men and women, and many distinguished people have visited the town. Princess Victoria came to Lyme with her mother, the Duchess of Kent, in August 1833, and during her reign her son, the Prince of Wales, stayed at The Royal Lion. The artist J. McNeil Whistler immortalized Lyme in his painting of the smith and smithy, and he, too, stayed at The Royal Lion. The geologists Buckland, Conybeare and De La Beche often met at The Assembly Rooms. Lord Lister, Lord Halsbury, Sir John Lubbock, Sir H. Beerbohm, Canon Fleming and Miss Ellen Terry are also among the many famous people who have visited the town over the years.

SIR GEORGE SOMERS

Sir George Somers was the son of John Somers of Lyme Regis. He was born in 1554 and became a sailor. Wanklyn describes him as a buccaneering Elizabethan sailor. He did in fact take part in various expeditions to the West Indies and America, as well as Raleigh's expedition to the Azores in 1609. He was MP for Lyme in 1602, knighted by James I in 1603 and Mayor of Lyme in 1604. With the Earl of Southampton and others he was one of the founders of the South Virginia Company, and he was the naval commander of an expedition to take new settlers to the colony.

The fleet set sail in May 1609, Somers travelling in the 300 ton flagship *Seaventure*. *Seaventure* was driven away from the rest of the fleet during a hurricane that July and was eventually driven ashore in the Bermudas, the fleet having continued safely to Virginia. Somers and his ship's company miraculously escaped destruction, as the *Seaventure*, when driven ashore, lodged upright between two rocks. All got safely ashore with all of the goods in the ship. Good food and water were found in plenty on the island, and life there proved to be so pleasant that some of the crew refused to leave. Sir George Somers, the other officers and some of the crew eventually, after ten months, got away from the island in two pinnaces that they had built, and they arrived in Virginia in May 1610, having previously taken formal possession of the Bermudas in the name of James I. Somers later died there of

Berne Farm, Whitchurch Canonicorum, *c.* 1920. This was the house owned by Sir George Somers at the time of his death in 1610

a surfeit of pig and his heart was buried there. His body was buried in the church at Whitchurch Canonicorum beneath the old chantry, a fact recorded on a brass tablet on the south wall of the present vestry.

SIR EDMUND PRIDAUX

Another of Lyme's MPs important in national affairs was Sir Edmund Pridaux, a Chancery lawyer who became Cromwell's Attorney-General and was knighted. He represented Lyme in Parliament for nineteen years and was recorder for the borough in 1655. He sat throughout the Long Parliament and was still MP for Lyme when he died in 1659. His first colleague in the representation of the borough was Richard Rose who, earlier, had been Mayor of Lyme. Rose was a determined Radical and an outspoken opponent of ship-money. When he heard that the Royal Navy was going to cruise in the English Channel to maintain Charles's title of 'King of the Narrow Seas', he was reported to the Privy Council as having said, in 1637, 'What foolery is this, that the country in general should be taxed with great sums to maintain the King's titles and honours?' Even in those days there were people too stupid to see that the well-being of the country as a whole depended on the Navy and on the prestige of its sovereign in the eyes of the world. Rose was buried in Lyme Regis parish church.

The last of Pridaux's colleagues as MP for Lyme was Henry Henley. Henley was lord of the manor and a member of the family that controlled elections at Lyme Regis, to a limited extent, until displaced by the Fane family. Pridaux, prior to his appointment as Attorney-General, had been Master of the Posts and had established a post between London and Lyme in 1644 for the conveyance of intelligence from western parts. He greatly improved the postal service and was also able to make £15,000 a year for himself! Before he died he had acquired Forde Abbey, which later became the residence of his son.

The younger Edmund Pridaux got into trouble in 1682 and again later. He was MP for Taunton and, referring to the redemption of English captives enslaved by Muslims, had said, or was alleged to have said, that it was 'better to live in slavery under the Turks than in England under Popery'. In his report of the incident, Gregory Alford of Lyme, the Royalist accuser, referred to Pridaux as 'the little Parliament-man for Taunton and son of Oliver's Attorney-General'. Alford said that Pridaux's house had formerly been an abbey. In it was 'a chapel wherein preaches a Nonconformist. It is the receptacle of all the Fanatics.' Three years later, after the Monmouth affair, Pridaux was arrested and imprisoned in the Tower of London, because some of Monmouth's troops had called at Forde Abbey and had drunk the duke's health. Pridaux is said to have had to purchase his freedom from Judge Jeffreys at a cost of £15,000.

CAPTAIN THOMAS CORAM, C. 1688–1751

Thomas Coram, a native of Lyme Regis, created The Foundling Hospital in London in the eighteenth century. He was born in about 1688 and became a sailor like his father before him. He traded with Virginia and lived for a time in the American colonies. On his return to England he was consulted about the colonization of Georgia and Nova Scotia and he played a prominent part in the settlement of both. In about 1720 he was engaged in the supply of stores to the Navy. His work often took him into some of the worst of the Thames-side districts below London Bridge, where many deserted children were to be seen about the streets, dying or dead through parental neglect. Many of them were the unwanted children of unmarried mothers – women such as Moll Flanders, perhaps.

Coram's sympathies were easily aroused for he was fond of children. He determined to create a home for at least some of them. Though not a wealthy man he had done reasonably well for himself, and he spent twenty years of his life and all of his money in bringing The Foundling Hospital into being. He met with much apathy, obstruction and ridicule, but in the end managed to obtain a Royal Charter and to collect enough funds to make a start. First he bought a house in Hatton Garden. Then he bought an estate in Lamb's Conduit Fields for £6,500, and The Foundling Hospital was opened there in

Thomas Coram who was born in Coombe Street

1745. (The property was sold in the 1920s for £1,650,000.) Hogarth, who painted Coram's portrait, was one of the original governors of the hospital. Money was raised by holding art exhibitions there, an enterprise that is said to have been the forerunner of the Royal Academy.

Handel, too, was a generous benefactor of the hospital. One of the ways in which he helped was to conduct annual performances of *Messiah* in the chapel. Thousands of pounds were raised in this way. The original score of the oratorio became one of the hospital's most valued possessions. Eventually Coram, who had become an old man and did not always see eye to eye with his colleagues, was ousted from his position on the council. He had ruined himself for the sake of the hospital and was in financial difficulties. A subscription was raised and an annuity bought for him in 1749. Mr Smith, the rector of Allhallows-on-the-Wall and occasional chaplain to The Foundling Hospital, gave a home to the old captain in this time of adversity. In October 1749, by a unanimous vote, the corporation conferred on him the freedom of the borough of Lyme Regis. The letter in which Coram acknowledged the compliment is in The Lyme Museum. It was written from Mr Smith's house. Two years later Coram died and was buried in a vault beneath the chapel of his hospital.

MARY ANNING, 1799–1847

Mary Anning was the eldest child of Richard Anning, a carpenter and a Dissenter of Lyme Regis. Anning supplemented his income by gathering and selling fossils to visitors. Mary often accompanied him and learned where to look for fossils and how to deal with them. Her father died in 1810 and Mary began to help her mother to support the family by taking over her father's enterprise. As a result her schooling apparently ceased. Among her customers were the geologists de la Beche and Colonel Birch, and also the lord of the manor, H.H. Henley.

Mary Anning's first important discovery was made in 1811. It was the first associated skeleton of an Ichthyosaurus ever found in anything approaching a complete condition. Mary engaged workmen to extract the fossil from the rock and, according to Roberts, sold it to Henley for £23. Henley gave it to Bullock's Museum. It is said to be in the Natural History Museum now. Mary thus became known to eminent geologists, who included William Buckland, the first Professor of Geology in the University of Oxford, and William Daniel Conybeare. Buckland, who was born at Axminster in 1784 and became Dean of Westminster in 1845, frequently went fossil-hunting with Mary.

Mary became acquainted with Conybeare through her discovery, in 1824, of an almost complete skeleton of Plesiosaurus, the first to be found. Earlier Conybeare and de la Beche had jointly written an account, based on skeletal fragments found in various collections, of this marine reptile. Then Conybeare described Mary's Plesiosaurus in *Transactions of the Geological Society*, and the fossil was placed in the smaller reptile gallery of the British Museum. Some of the fragments were found at Lyme by Colonel Birch, or bought by him from Mary.

Conybeare was born in 1787 and died in 1857. He married Sarah Anne Ranken in 1814 and they had seven sons and two daughters. Conybeare became rector of Sully Glamorgan and then, in 1831, was appointed to Axminster. He was Dean of Llandaff until his death. He and Buckland frequently worked together, for Conybeare was an enthusiastic geologist and wrote a treatise on the subject.

Mary Anning's third important discovery, in December 1828, was the skeleton of the flying reptile Pterodactyl, a species hitherto unknown. The fossil was described by Buckland and was acquired by the British Museum. Soon afterwards Mary found a specimen of a new kind of Plesiosaurus – Macrocephalus. She wrote to Buckland about it in 1830. He described it and it was acquired by the British Museum.

Yet another geologist, Thomas Hawkins, worked at Lyme with Mary, in 1832. Later Hawkins wrote the following tribute to her:

This lady, devoting herself to Science, explored the frowning and precipitous cliffs, when the furious spring tide conspired with the howling tempest to overthrow them, and rescued from the gaping ocean, sometimes at the peril of her life, the few specimens which originated all the fact and ingenious theories of these persons (the great geologists) whose names must ever be remembered with sentiments of the liveliest gratitude.

In 1844 Mary also assisted the King of Saxony in collecting fossils. She died of cancer at the age of forty-seven.

JANE AUSTEN, 1775–1817

For enthusiastic readers of the novels of Jane Austen, 'Granny's Teeth' must be one of the more interesting landmarks in Lyme. Jane enjoyed a holiday in Lyme in 1804, and called on her happy memories when, twelve years later, she wrote her novel *Persuasion*. 'Granny's Teeth' is the name given to the peculiar set of granite blocks projecting from The Cobb wall and forming steps to the upper parapet. In *Persuasion* they are the setting for Louisa Musgrove's unfortunate accident – she attempted to jump down into the arms of Captain Wentworth, but missed and lay insensible on The Cobb. The

'Granny's Teeth', The Cobb, *c.* 1946. These are the steps from which Louisa Musgrove fell in Jane Austen's book *Persuasion*

house where she was taken to recover, the Harville lodging, was Bay Cottage on Marine Parade. Wings, where Louisa was lodging, was also on Marine Parade, but was demolished just after the Second World War. Lord Tennyson visited Lyme in 1867 to see the steps from which Louisa Musgrove fell.

There is some speculation that Jane herself had a romance while she was staying in Lyme and that that of Anne Elliot in *Persuasion* was based on this experience. She and her mother would also have visited The Assembly Rooms, demolished in 1929, which would have given her plenty of material for later scenes and characters. It is easy to imagine how the Regency charm of Lyme would have appealed to her, and it is still possible to see many of the features that were quite new at that time.

In a letter to her sister during her stay in Lyme, Jane spoke of the bathing being 'delightful' and also mentioned seeing Richard Anning collecting fossils with his daughter. Mary Anning would have been five at the time. It is quite possible that Jane and her sisters also searched for fossils on the beach.

DR WILLIAM DIXON LANG FRS, 1878–1966

The geologist William Lang was an acknowledged expert on the stratigraphy of Dorset. He published many learned papers and produced detailed maps, at a scale of 25 inches to the mile, of west Dorset. These important maps, which were published by The Geological Society, gave new insight into the geology of the region and have been widely studied.

Lang was born in India and educated in England, reading Natural Sciences at Cambridge and graduating in 1902. He spent his working life in London in the Geological Department at the British Museum. He continued with his research and over the years published many important papers, on both the stratigraphy of Dorset and, his other main interest, corals and their evolution. He went on to become keeper in 1928 and was elected a Fellow of the Royal Society in 1929.

In 1898 Lang visited Charmouth for a holiday and found the area much to his liking. There he met a local woman, Catherine Dixon, who became his wife in 1908. They spent all of their spare time in west Dorset, and it was during these visits that Lang spent so much time painstakingly preparing his maps, beginning with Charmouth and working west to Lyme Regis and east to Seatown. The mapping required meticulous work, and he was usually to be found by the cliffs, notebook and compass clinometer in hand. The area was ideal for this type of detailed study owing to the outstandingly good exposure of the lower lias sedimentary rocks.

When Lang retired in 1938 he and his family moved to Charmouth, where he spent many happy hours in the countryside and on the beach. He

Cobb Hamlet, 1927. Dr Wingrave lived in a house by the beach (second from right)

continued to write papers, both on geology and on many aspects of natural history. He was able to take a very active role in the Dorset Natural History and Archaeological Society, and served as its president in 1938. He was well liked and respected for his wide knowledge of the area, and was always ready to help to solve problems and assist with the identification of specimens.

DR V. WYATT WINGRAVE MD, MR,CS, LSA

Wyatt Wingrave was a native of Coventry. He studied for his degree in London and became a throat and ear specialist at the Central London Throat and Ear Hospital, where he served for thirty years. It was here, when dealing with a diphtheria patient, that he lost the sight in his left eye, became totally deaf and partially paralysed. In spite of this he refused to give up his medical work.

With determination he overcame his physical disabilities, continued his lectures and devoted himself to pathology. He was a lecturer on physiology at the School of Anatomy and a lecturer at the Medical Graduates College and the Polyclinic. He was for a time president of the British Laryngological Society and wrote a number of medical books on diseases of the ear and throat. During the 1914–18 war Wingrave carried out pathological work for five London hospitals, and soon after the Armistice he came to reside permanently at Lyme Regis. He brought his fossils and specimens with him, and in 1922 founded the Lyme Regis Museum. He became the first curator, retiring in 1935 through ill-health.

In 1935 his life of devoted service to humanity was recognized when the Freedom of the City of Coventry was conferred on him. This was followed by the Freedom of Lyme Regis, shortly before his death in 1938, to honour his geological work and other efforts for the benefit of Lyme Regis Museum. He devoted most of his leisure time to the collection of fossils, and these were presented to the museum.

DR ERNEST LE CRONIER LANCASTER

Ernest Lancaster was one of the distinguished group of people who came to live in Lyme Regis between the two wars. Before his retirement he was consultant surgeon at the Swansea Hospital and curator of the Swansea Museum.

Mr and Mrs Rowe, *c.* 1908. Mr Rowe was a staunch member of the Lyme Regis Wesleyan church, where he was also a preacher. He lived at 55 Church Street and was a much respected member of the local community

At Lyme Regis Lancaster identified himself with the Philpot Museum, where he became curator until his death in 1945 at the age of eighty-four. He lived at Penard in Colway Lane, and was a noted naturalist and an authority on shellfish and molluscs.

JOHN FOWLES, 1926–

One of the most talented of contemporary British authors, John Fowles, has made his home in Lyme Regis, the town that he used as the setting for *The French Lieutenant's Woman*. He was born in 1926 in Leigh-on-Sea in Essex, and first lived in the West Country when he was evacuated to a small village called Ippleden. *The Collector*, Fowles's first novel, was an immediate success, and collectors will pay up to £200 for a first edition of the book, complete with dust jacket.

Fowles's third novel, *The French Lieutenant's Woman*, was filmed in Lyme, and Meryl Streep gave a memorable performance in the title role of the film when she played Sarah Woodruff. The novel was set in the Lyme Regis of 1860, and the image of Meryl Streep standing on the windswept Cobb is the scene we all remember. John Fowles has contributed much to Lyme, becoming the curator of the local museum and publishing two books on the town.

CHAPTER EIGHT

The Cobb

There is no obvious reason for The Cobb to be situated where it is, not being sited at a natural harbour or estuary, but it is believed to date from the early thirteenth century. The earliest documentary evidence of its existence is from 1328, when a document states that it was built of timber and rocks. In 1825, when the tide was abnormally low and extensive rebuilding was in progress, it was possible to see the remains of a structure of three rows of piles supported by large rocks, just inside the line of the outer Cobb wall. It was always vulnerable to south-west gales, and all or parts of it have been destroyed many times over the centuries.

The Hon. Roger North described his visit to Lyme in the late seventeenth century. He said that Lyme 'is situate in the cod of a bay, where there is no river or land-lock provided by nature to prevent the certain loss of ships at anchor there; and, of all places upon the coast of England, least to be suspected for a good port'. He continued:

The harbour and The Cobb, *c.* 1910

But art and industry will do wonders; for all the requisites of a safe harbour are supplied by this Cob. The small vessels which serve the trade of the town, consisting chiefly in woollen manufactures of that country, carry on the trade outwards, which is very beneficial. And in that respect King Charles II allowed out of the customs of that port £100 per annum towards the charge of maintaining the Cob. The Cob is a mole built in the sea, about two furlongs from the town, and named from the cobble-stone of which it is compiled. It is an immense mass of stone, of the shape of a demilune, with a bar in the middle of the concave: no one stone that lies there was ever touched with a tool or is bedded in any sort of cement, but all being pebbles of the sea are piled up, and held by their bearings only, and the surge plays in and out through the interstices of the stone in a wonderful manner. That this must often decay is certain: but there is warning enough to alarm the town to repair . . . for sometimes a swamp will appear in the flat top where they walk: and they go to work and take down all that part, and build it up from the bottom, and nothing less will prevent the downfall of much more as the seas rage against it. And it may happen that some new foundation stones are to be laid. These are the largest sort that can be got, and they search them out upon the coast. Mounting them upon casks chained together, with but one man mounted upon them, he with the help of a pole conducts it to the place where it is to lie: and then, striking out an iron pin, away go the casks and the stone falls in its place.

The vessels of burthen are laden and unladen by horses, turning and

The Cobb, *c.* 1880

The harbour, *c.* 1900

returning upon the sand between the Cob and the town. They have no drivers but are charged with bales, for instance, at the warehouse and away they trot to the ship's side and stand fair, sometimes above the belly in water, for the tackle to discharge them, and then they gallop back to the warehouses for more. And so they perform the tide's work and know by the flood when their labour is at an end.

Before the storm of 1817 the greater part of The Cobb was built in this way, and wedges were sometimes driven in as a holding measure when any part of the wall began to bulge out. The outer pier swept away by the storm of 1792 was replaced to roughly the original length, but not on the old plan of building. Portland capstone, in blocks weighing five tons in some cases, was used for the exterior; cow-stones (cobblestones) were used to fill the interior. The large blocks were fastened together 'by pices of iron fixed in a groove and cemented by having boiling lead poured at the ends to fasten the iron cramp'.

A record of the reconstruction of the extreme part of the outer wall may be seen, carved on a stone in the parapet wall, at The Cobb. It states: 'The work extending 273 feet west of this stone was erected by James Hamilton, builder

A view from The Cobb, *c.* 1885

and contractor with the honourable Board of Ordnance, to repair the
breaches made in the Cobb in January 1792, under the direction of Captain
D'Arcy, engineer, 1795.' This was only part of the reconstruction. The other
part, extending from this inscription to the extreme seaward end of The
Cobb, was carried out under the direction of Major D'Aubant.

The storm of 1792 was followed twenty-five years later (on 20 January
1817) by another, which destroyed the part of the old wall from a little east of
the slip to the present steps by the brass plate. In 1818 the Committee of
Repairs in the House of Commons enquired into the repair work then
required, and considered whether The Cobb should be treated as a national
work. The conclusions reached were that this harbour was the best in the bay,
that at high water in spring tides it was open to vessels of 120 to 150 tons
with a draught of 14 feet and that in some respects it was preferable to bar
harbours along the coast when a violent onshore wind was accompanied by a
high sea. A further consideration was that the cattle trade between the west of
England and the Channel Islands depended on the peculiar position of the
harbour, which made it accessible in winds that prevented entrance into other
parts of West Bay. This trade was very important during the Napoleonic
Wars. In November 1815 Thomas Walker, master of the *Active*, made four
voyages when vessels from other ports could not go to sea.

A grant was made by government and Colonel Fanshaw began the
reconstruction. He rebuilt the main body of The Cobb up to the level of the
bottom of the parapet wall but, owing to government economies, it was left
to the Lyme Corporation to rebuild the parapet wall in stages, as and when

they could afford it. This was at a time when the Fane family still controlled the corporation. Only two courses of heavy Portland stone had been laid above Colonel Fanshaw's work when the great storm of 23 November 1824 swept away not only those, but also Fanshaw's upper courses.

George Roberts, the local historian, gave an eyewitness account of the event. After a fine autumn the weather became stormy and the wind blew a hurricane from the south.

> At one a.m. on Tuesday 23rd the tide was flowing . . . At three the tide came up to high water mark, neap tides: this was five hours before the time of high water! Before four it had risen to a great height; and some persons who were about, to look after their boats . . . forewarned individuals at the Cobb houses of the danger. Soon after, the sea broke over the walls, and the inmates were with difficulty taken out. The sea-walls which protect several houses in the lowest part of the town, near the mouth of the river, and on the walk, were destroyed.
>
> Between the showers the gusts of wind were tremendous and were accompanied by thunder and lightning. Chimneys were blown down, and other mischief done. At day-break I saw the sea from the Bell Cliff, and clearly distinguished a violence in the gale, and in the height of the water, beyond anything I had before witnessed. About six or seven a great breach took place in the Cobb, when the sea ran through in a manner truly appalling and soon swept every vessel out. Two men in the revenue tender

PS Victoria at Lyme Regis, *c.* 1913

were drowned. The *Unity*, a London trader ready for sea, was driven with her crew to Charmouth beach: the crew were lashed to the shrouds and were saved at low water. All the stones laid by the corporation in the parapet, and part of Col. Fanshawe's upper courses, were swept away.

All the old work, between the new work to near the Gin-shop, in length 232 feet, was thrown down: the northern wall, the Crab-head, and the quay, were much injured, and a scene of devastation was presented that defies description . . . The warehouses on the Cobb suffered much. The largest was destroyed. An old man and his wife were in their little dwelling house near the Crab-head . . . They saved themselves by getting out at the back of their dwelling, and then into a window of the watch-house belonging to the customs, where the man scuttled the floor and saved the house: his dwelling was destroyed.

The work of rebuilding The Cobb began on 19 April 1825 and proceeded with spirit, sometimes by torchlight, as the weather was favourable. It was completed on 18 November 1826. On a brass plate at The Cobb it is stated that the length of pier rebuilt was 232 feet and the length of parapet 447 feet. This work was carried out under the direction of Lieutenant-Colonel Fanshaw RE and under the immediate superintendence of Captain Savage RE. The method of construction involved laying very deep foundations, particularly on the seaward side. The interior was of cow-stone, worked and carefully laid, with occasional bonding courses of capstone. The exterior was made up of solid Portland capstone laid in courses. The courses were joined together by iron bolts let into the blocks. Each block in a course was bound to the next by dovetails of heart of oak in preference to iron cramps.

A painting of The Cobb, *c.* 1820

The reconstruction cost much money. In 1794 the government contributed £10,002 5s. 0d. From 1818 to 1825 it had contributed a total of £32,629 3s. 1d. It is evident that the harbour was valued as a work of national importance.

With each major rebuilding The Cobb was changed in shape. Originally it was a 'V' shape, with a straight side parallel to the shore and closed at the west end. It was not until 1756 that there was a causeway connecting it with the shore. The quay was originally very narrow, but a low causeway, dry only at low tide, ran along its length. The present wider quay covers this causeway.

The Customs House was rebuilt in 1700, just above the old fish market and across the road from Cobb Gate. This building was burned down in 1844. The new Customs House was erected at the bottom of Cobb Road, on a site later occupied by a house called Cobb Lodge. 1845 was rather late to be building a new Customs House as not only was the import and export trade in Lyme decreasing, but soon after free trade was introduced.

There was a shipbuilding yard to the west of The Cobb where shipbuilding was recorded from the late thirteenth century. A frigate for the Navy was built there in 1654. In the mid-nineteenth century the owner was John Mansfield, the last of a long succession of shipwrights. The *Lyme Regis*, a ship of 250 tons, was launched in 1849 by Lady Bayly, and this was a day of great celebration in the town. John Mansfield built two more vessels, both of about 700 tons, before he retired in around 1854. In about 1830 Drayton, the Mayor of Lyme, built the bonding yards at the corner of Cobb Road and the Walk. Drayton stored his foreign timber there.

The Cobb saw its last commercial transactions in the 1930s when it was being used for the import of timber and cement. There were always pleasure trips for the summer visitors, and earlier in the century small paddle-steamers brought trippers from Weymouth and Exmouth. The Cobb continues to require regular inspection and maintenance, since the strength of the sea could quickly cause considerable damage. Lyme still supports a small fishing fleet, besides providing mooring for many recreation and pleasure craft.

Acknowledgements

We are grateful to all who have contributed information for this book. Particular thanks are owed to John Godfrey and Peter Cousins for the loan of photographs, and to the *Bridport News* for allowing us access to their archives. Thanks must also go to Gerald Gosling, Norman Whinfrey and Edna Everitt, who gave much-appreciated help. We are also grateful to Geoff Marshall and Carol Gosling for their encouragement, and to Simon Thraves for his assistance. The accuracy of the facts in this book have been checked as carefully as possible. However, original sources can contain errors, and memories fade over the years. We should be happy to receive further information on the history of the area.

Ted Gosling and Lyn Marshall

The British Isles in Old Photographs

BERKSHIRE
* Maidenhead
* Around Windsor
* Slough
* Around Thatcham
* Reading: A Second Selection
* Sandhurst and Crowthorne
* Reading
  Windsor

BUCKINGHAMSHIRE
* High Wycombe

CORNWALL
* The Lower Fal Estuary
* Around Truro
* Penzance and Newlyn
  Falmouth

CUMBERLAND
* Around Whitehaven

DERBYSHIRE
* Derby

DEVON
* Seaton, Lyme Regis and Axminster
* Honiton and the Otter Valley
  Around Tiverton
  Kingsbridge
  Exeter
  From Haldon to Mid-Dartmoor
  Devon and Cornwall Railways
  Around Topsham: Countess Wear to Lympstone
  Around Seaton and Sidmouth

DORSET
* Around Gillingham
  Around Blandford Forum
  Bournemouth
  Swanage and Purbeck

DURHAM
* Darlington: A Second Selection
  Darlington
  Houghton-Le-Spring and Hetton-Le-Hole
  Houghton-Le-Spring and Hetton-Le-Hole: A Second Selection
  Teesdale
  Durham City
  Weardale
  Around Darlington
  Sunderland

DYFED
  Aberystwyth and North Ceredigion
  Haverfordwest
  Upper Tywi Valley
  Cardigan and the Lower Teifi Valley

  The Haven
  Lampeter and the Upper Teifi Valley

ESSEX
  Colchester

GLOUCESTERSHIRE
  The Forest of Dean
  Stroud and the Five Valleys
  The Forest of Dean: A Second Selection
* Gloucester
  The Severn Vale
  Cirencester
  Thornbury to Berkeley
  Wotton-Under-Edge to Chipping Sodbury
  Fairford and Lechlade
  Northleach to Stow-On-The-Wold
  Around Gloucester
  Stonehouse to Painswick
  Tetbury, Nailsworth and Minchinhampton
  The Forest: Dean Heritage Museum
  Bishop's Cleeve and Winchcombe
  Tewkesbury and the Vale of Gloucester
  Cheltenham: A Second Selection
  The North Cotswolds
  Stroud & The Five Valleys: A Second Selection
  Stroud Road and Rail
  Around Bishop's Cleeve and Winchcombe
  Gloucester: From the Walwin Collection
  Stroudwater and Thames & Severn Canals
  Stroud's Golden Valley
  Churn, Coln and Leach Valleys
  Uley, Dursley and Cam
  Around Cirencester

GWYNEDD
  Around Llandudno
* Anglesey
  Gwynedd Railways
  The Vale of Conwy

HAMPSHIRE
  Hampshire Railways
  Portsmouth
  Gosport

HEREFORDSHIRE
* Herefordshire

KENT
* Early Broadstairs and St Peter's
* Margate
* Folkestone: A Second Selection
* Lympne Airport
  Maidstone
* Gravesend
  Broadstairs and St Peter's
* Bexley
  Sittingbourne

Faversham
Ramsgate and Thanet Life
Greenwich and Woolwich
Canterbury
Tunbridge Wells
Deal
Chatham and Gillingham
* Goudhurst to Tenterden
Folkestone
Around Gravesham
Herne Bay
Around Tonbridge
RAF Hawkinge
* Eltham

LANCASHIRE
Lancashire North of the Sands
* North Fylde

LEICESTERSHIRE
Charnwood Forest
* Around Melton Mowbray
* The River Soar
Harborough In Camera
Around The Welland Valley

LINCOLNSHIRE
Scunthorpe
* Skegness
* Around Grimsby
Grimsby
Around Louth

LONDON
Hackney
Lewisham and Deptford
* Lewisham and Deptford: A Second Selection
Hackney: A Second Selection

MONMOUTHSHIRE
* Chepstow and the River Wye
Monmouth and the River Wye

NORFOLK
Norwich

NOTTINGHAMSHIRE
* Victorian Nottingham
Around Newark
Arnold and Bestwood
* Nottingham: 1944–1974

OXFORDSHIRE
* Witney District
* Around Henley-on-Thames
* Bicester and Otmoor
Burford
Banbury
Banburyshire

Around Abingdon
Witney
Around Chipping Norton
Wantage, Faringdon and the Vale Villages
Oxford: The University
Around Woodstock
Around Chipping Norton: A Second Selection
Oxfordshire Railways
Oxfordshire Railways: A Second Selection
Around Witney
Around Didcot and The Hagbournes

SCOTLAND
Clydesdale
Selkirkshire

SOMERSET
* Chard and Ilminster
* Bath
* Weston-Super-Mare
Bristol
Keynsham and Saltford
Midsomer Norton and Radstock
* Around Weston-Super-Mare
Taunton
Wells
Clevedon
Around Burnham-On-Sea and Highbridge
The Mendips
Around Bath
Weston-Super-Mare: The 1950s
West Somerset Villages

STAFFORDSHIRE
* Wednesfield and Heath Town
Walsall
Bilston
Around Rugeley
Penkridge to Brewood
Wednesbury, Tipton and Darlaston
* Smethwick
West Bromwich
Around Cannock
Penn
Around Tettenhall and Codsall
Around Stafford
Black Country Pubs
* Wombourne and Pattingham
Aldridge
Oldbury and Rowley Regis

SUFFOLK
* Around Woodbridge
Ipswich
Southwold to Aldeburgh
Around Ipswich

SURREY
* Farnham: A Second Selection
* Around Epsom
* Surrey At Work
  Dorking
  Around Farnham
  Richmond
  Around Haslemere and Hindhead

SUSSEX
* RAF Tangmere
  Goodwood Country
  Around Rye
  Brighton and Hove
  Haywards Heath
* Hastings
  Eastbourne
  Bexhill-On-Sea
  Bognor Regis
  Arundel and The Arun Valley
  The High Weald
  Around Heathfield
  Around Crawley
  Littlehampton
  Lewes
  Chichester
  Hastings: A Second Selection
  Around Heathfield: A Second Selection
  Around Hailsham
  Bishopstone and Seaford
  Around Worthing

WARWICKSHIRE
  Around Leamington Spa
* Birmingham Railways
  Nuneaton
  Bedworth
  The Stour Valley
  Around Bulkington
  Around Warwick
  Victorian Stratford-Upon-Avon
  Around Coventry

WESTMORLAND
  South Westmorland Villages
  Kendal
* The Eden Valley
  The Westmorland Lakes

WILTSHIRE
  Around Highworth
* Castle Combe to Malmesbury
* Salisbury: A Third Selection
  Trowbridge
  Salisbury
  Westbury
  Swindon
  The Wylye Valley
  The Pewsey Vale
* Salisbury: A Second Selection
  Around Devizes
  Around Calne
  Around Westbury
  Warminster
  Swindon: A Second Selection
  Around Salisbury
  Around Melksham
  Marlborough: A Second Selection
  Around Amesbury
  Around Wootton Bassett, Cricklade and Purton
  Corsham and Box
  Swindon: A Third Selection
  Around Wilton
  Chippenham and Lacock

WORCESTERSHIRE
* Around Worcester
* Worcester
  Droitwich
  Around Pershore
  Worcester In A Day
  Evesham to Bredon
  Around Malvern
  Around Droitwich
  Redditch and The Needle District

YORKSHIRE
  Skipton and The Dales
  Scarborough's War Years
  Around Richmond
  Huddersfield
  Huddersfield: A Second Selection
  Scarborough
  Around Skipton

Price £7.95 and £7.99★

All of these titles are available from your local bookseller or direct from
Alan Sutton Publishing, Phoenix Mill, Far Thrupp, Stroud, Gloucestershire,
GL5 2BU
Tel: (0453) 731114 Fax: (0453) 731117 Sales and trade counter: 0453 731115